The Poetry of Alexander Pope

Volume VII

Alexander Pope was born on May 21st, 1688 in London into a Catholic family.

His education was affected by the recent Test Acts, upholding the status of the Church of England and banning Catholics from teaching. In effect this meant his formal education was over by the age of 12 and Pope was to now immerse himself in classical literature and languages and to, in effect, educate himself.

From this age too he also suffered from numerous health problems including a type of tuberculosis (Pott's disease) which resulted in a stunted, deformed body. Only to grow to a height of 4' 6", with a severe hunchback and complicated further by respiratory difficulties, high fevers, inflamed eyes and abdominal pain all of which served to further isolate him, initially, from society.

However his talent was evident to all. Best known for his satirical verse, his translations of Homer and the use of the heroic couplet, he is the second-most frequently quoted writer in The Oxford Dictionary of Quotations, after Shakespeare.

With the publication of Pastorals in 1709 followed by An Essay on Criticism (1711) and his most famous work The Rape of the Lock (1712; revised and enlarged in 1714) Pope became not only famous but wealthy.

His translations of the Iliad and the Odyssey further enhanced both reputation and purse. His engagement to produce an opulent new edition of Shakespeare met with a mixed reception. Pope attempted to "regularise" Shakespeare's metre and rewrote some of his verse and cut 1500 lines, that Pope considered to be beneath the Bard's standard, to mere footnotes.

Alexander Pope died on May 30th, 1744 at his villa at Twickenham (where he created his famous grotto and gardens) and was buried in the nave of the nearby Church of England Church of St Mary the Virgin.

Over the years and centuries since his death Pope's work has been in and out of favour but with this distance he is now truly recognised as one of England's greatest poets.

Index of Contents

MORAL ESSAYS.

The 'Essay on Man' was intended to have been comprised in four books:—

The first of which, the author has given us under that title, in four epistles.

The second was to have consisted of the same number:—1. Of the extent and limits of human reason. 2. Of those arts and sciences, and of the parts of them, which are useful, and therefore attainable, together with those which are unuseful, and therefore unattainable. 3. Of the nature, ends, use, and application of the different capacities of men. 4. Of the use of learning, of the science of the world, and of wit; concluding with a satire against the misapplication of them, illustrated by pictures, characters, and examples.

The third book regarded civil regimen, or the science of politics, in which the several forms of a republic were to have been examined and explained; together with the several modes of religious worship, as far forth as they affect society; between which the author always supposed there was the most interesting relation and closest connexion; so that this part would have treated of civil and religious society in their full extent.

The fourth and last book concerned private ethics or practical morality, considered in all the circumstances, orders, professions, and stations of human life.

The scheme of all this had been maturely digested, and communicated to the Lord Bolingbroke, Dr Swift, and one or two more, and was intended for the only work of his riper years; but was, partly through ill health, partly through discouragements from the depravity of the times, and partly on prudential and other considerations, interrupted, postponed, and, lastly, in a manner laid aside.

But as this was the author's favourite work, which more exactly reflected the image of his strong capacious mind, and as we can have but a very imperfect idea of it from the disjecta membra poetae that now remain, it may not be amiss to be a little more particular concerning each of these projected books. The first, as it treats of man in the abstract, and considers him in general under every one of his relations, becomes the foundation, and furnishes out the subjects, of the three following; so that—

The second book takes up again the first and second epistles of the first book, and treats of man in his intellectual capacity at large, as has been explained above. Of this, only a small part of the conclusion (which, as we said, was to have contained a satire against the misapplication of wit and learning) may be found in the fourth book of 'The Dunciad,' and up and down, occasionally, in the other three.

The third book, in like manner, reassumes the subject of the third epistle of the first, which treats of man in his social, political, and religious capacity. But this part the poet afterwards conceived might be best executed in an epic poem; as the action would make it more animated, and the fable less invidious; in which all the great principles of true and false governments and religions should be chiefly delivered in feigned examples.

The fourth and last book pursues the subject of the fourth epistle of the first, and treats of ethics, or practical morality; and would have consisted of many members; of which the four following epistles were detached portions: the two first, on the characters of men and women, being the introductory part of this concluding book.—Warburton.

EPISTLE I.—TO SIR RICHARD TEMPLE, LORD COBHAM.

ARGUMENT.

OF THE KNOWLEDGE AND CHARACTERS OF MEN.

That it is not sufficient for this knowledge to consider man in the abstract: books will not serve the purpose, nor yet our own experience singly, ver. 1. General maxims, unless they be formed upon both, will be but notional, ver. 10. Some peculiarity in every man, characteristic to himself, yet varying from himself, ver. 15. Difficulties arising from our own passions, fancies, faculties, &c., ver. 31. The shortness of life, to observe in, and the uncertainty of the principles of action in men, to observe by, ver. 37, &c. Our own principle of action often hid from ourselves, ver. 41. Some few characters plain, but in general confounded, dissembled, or inconsistent, ver. 51. The same man utterly different in different places and seasons, ver. 71. Unimaginable weaknesses in the greatest, ver. 70, &c. Nothing constant and certain but God and nature, ver. 95. No judging of the motives from the actions; the same actions proceeding from contrary motives, and the same motives influencing contrary actions, ver. 100. II. Yet to form characters, we can only take the strongest actions of a man's life, and try to make them agree: the utter uncertainty of this, from nature itself, and from policy, ver. 120. Characters given according to the rank of men of the world, ver. 135. And some reason for it, ver. 140. Education alters the nature, or at least character of many, ver. 149. Actions, passions, opinions, manners, humours, or principles, all subject to change. No judging by nature, from ver. 158 to 174. III. It only remains to find (if we can) his ruling passion: that will certainly influence all the rest, and can reconcile the seeming or real inconsistency of all his actions, ver. 175. Instanced in the extraordinary character of Clodio, ver. 179. A caution against mistaking second qualities for first, which will destroy all possibility of the knowledge of mankind, ver. 210. Examples of the strength of the ruling passion, and its continuation to the last breath, ver. 222, &c.

I.
Yes, you despise the man to books confined,
Who from his study rails at human kind;
Though what he learns he speaks, and may advance
Some general maxims, or be right by chance.
The coxcomb bird, so talkative and grave,
That from his cage cries 'Cuckold,' 'Whore,' and 'Knave,'
Though many a passenger he rightly call,

You hold him no philosopher at all.

And yet the fate of all extremes is such,
Men may be read, as well as books, too much.
To observations which ourselves we make,
We grow more partial for the observer's sake;
To written wisdom, as another's, less:
Maxims are drawn from notions, those from guess.
There's some peculiar in each leaf and grain,
Some unmark'd fibre, or some varying vein:
Shall only man be taken in the gross?
Grant but as many sorts of mind as moss.

That each from other differs, first confess;
Next that he varies from himself no less:
Add nature's, custom's, reason's, passion's strife,
And all opinion's colours cast on life.

Our depths who fathoms, or our shallows finds,
Quick whirls, and shifting eddies, of our minds?
On human actions reason though you can,
It may be reason, but it is not man:
His principle of action once explore,
That instant 'tis his principle no more.
Like following life through creatures you dissect,
You lose it in the moment you detect.

Yet more; the difference is as great between
The optics seeing, as the objects seen.
All manners take a tincture from our own;
Or come discolour'd, through our passions shown;
Or fancy's beam enlarges, multiplies,
Contracts, inverts, and gives ten thousand dyes.

Nor will life's stream for observation stay,
It hurries all too fast to mark their way:
In vain sedate reflections we would make,
When half our knowledge we must snatch, not take.
Oft, in the passions' wild rotation toss'd,
Our spring of action to ourselves is lost:
Tired, not determined, to the last we yield,
And what comes then is master of the field.
As the last image of that troubled heap,
When sense subsides, and fancy sports in sleep,
(Though past the recollection of the thought),
Becomes the stuff of which our dream is wrought:
Something as dim to our internal view,
Is thus, perhaps, the cause of most we do.

True, some are open, and to all men known;
Others so very close, they're hid from none;
(So darkness strikes the sense no less than light)
Thus gracious Chandos is beloved at sight;
And every child hates Shylock, though his soul
Still sits at squat, and peeps not from its hole.
At half mankind when generous Manly raves,
All know 'tis virtue, for he thinks them knaves:
When universal homage Umbra pays,
All see 'tis vice, and itch of vulgar praise.
When flattery glares, all hate it in a queen,
While one there is who charms us with his spleen.

But these plain characters we rarely find;
Though strong the bent, yet quick the turns of mind:
Or puzzling contraries confound the whole;
Or affectations quite reverse the soul.
The dull, flat falsehood serves for policy;
And, in the cunning, truth itself's a lie:
Unthought-of frailties cheat us in the wise;
The fool lies hid in inconsistencies.

See the same man, in vigour, in the gout;
Alone, in company; in place, or out;
Early at business, and at hazard late;
Mad at a fox-chase, wise at a debate;
Drunk at a borough, civil at a ball;
Friendly at Hackney, faithless at Whitehall.

Catius is ever moral, ever grave,
Thinks who endures a knave, is next a knave,
Save just at dinner—then prefers, no doubt,
A rogue with venison to a saint without.

Who would not praise Patricio's high desert,
His hand unstain'd, his uncorrupted heart,
His comprehensive head, all interests weigh'd,
All Europe saved, yet Britain not betray'd?
He thanks you not, his pride is in picquet,
Newmarket fame, and judgment at a bet.

What made (says Montaigne, or more sage Charron)
Otho a warrior, Cromwell a buffoon?
A perjured prince a leaden saint revere,
A godless regent tremble at a star?
The throne a bigot keep, a genius quit,
Faithless through piety, and duped through wit?

Europe a woman, child, or dotard rule,
And just her wisest monarch made a fool?

Know, God and Nature only are the same:
In man, the judgment shoots at flying game;
A bird of passage! gone as soon as found,
Now in the moon perhaps, now under ground.

II.
In vain the sage, with retrospective eye,
Would from the apparent what conclude the why,
Infer the motive from the deed, and show
That what we chanced was what we meant to do.
Behold! if fortune or a mistress frowns,
Some plunge in business, others shave their crowns:
To ease the soul of one oppressive weight,
This quits an empire, that embroils a state:
The same adust complexion has impell'd
Charles to the convent, Philip to the field.

Not always actions show the man: we find
Who does a kindness, is not therefore kind;
Perhaps prosperity becalm'd his breast,
Perhaps the wind just shifted from the east:
Not therefore humble he who seeks retreat,
Pride guides his steps, and bids him shun the great:
Who combats bravely is not therefore brave,
He dreads a death-bed like the meanest slave:
Who reasons wisely is not therefore wise,
His pride in reasoning, not in acting, lies.

But grant that actions best discover man;
Take the most strong, and sort them as you can:
The few that glare, each character must mark,
You balance not the many in the dark.
What will you do with such as disagree?
Suppress them, or miscall them policy?
Must then at once (the character to save)
The plain rough hero turn a crafty knave?
Alas! in truth the man but changed his mind,
Perhaps was sick, in love, or had not dined.
Ask why from Britain Cæsar would retreat?
Cæsar himself might whisper he was beat.
Why risk the world's great empire for a punk?
Cæsar perhaps might answer he was drunk.
But, sage historians! 'tis your task to prove
One action, conduct; one, heroic love.

'Tis from high life high characters are drawn;
A saint in crape is twice a saint in lawn;
A judge is just, a chancellor juster still;
A gownman, learn'd; a bishop, what you will;
Wise, if a minister; but, if a king,
More wise, more learn'd, more just, more everything,
Court-virtues bear, like gems, the highest rate,
Born where Heaven's influence scarce can penetrate:
In life's low vale, the soil the virtues like,
They please as beauties, here as wonders strike.
Though the same sun with all-diffusive rays
Blush in the rose, and in the diamond blaze,
We prize the stronger effort of his power,
And justly set the gem above the flower.

'Tis education forms the common mind,
Just as the twig is bent, the tree's inclined.
Boastful and rough, your first son is a squire;
The next a tradesman, meek, and much a liar;
Tom struts a soldier, open, bold, and brave;
Will sneaks a scrivener, an exceeding knave:
Is he a Churchman? then he's fond of power:
A Quaker? sly: A Presbyterian? sour:
A smart free-thinker? all things in an hour.
Ask men's opinions: Scoto now shall tell
How trade increases, and the world goes well;
Strike off his pension, by the setting sun,
And Britain, if not Europe, is undone.

That gay free-thinker, a fine talker once,
What turns him now a stupid silent dunce?
Some god, or spirit he has lately found;
Or chanced to meet a minister that frown'd.

Judge we by nature? Habit can efface,
Interest o'ercome, or policy take place:
By actions? those uncertainty divides:
By passions? these dissimulation hides:
Opinions? they still take a wider range:
Find, if you can, in what you cannot change.

Manners with fortunes, humours turn with climes,
Tenets with books, and principles with times.

III.
Search, then, the ruling passion: there, alone,
The wild are constant, and the cunning known;
The fool consistent, and the false sincere;

Priests, princes, women, no dissemblers here.
This clue once found, unravels all the rest,
The prospect clears, and Wharton stands confess'd.
Wharton, the scorn and wonder of our days,
Whose ruling passion was the lust of praise:
Born with whate'er could win it from the wise,
Women and fools must like him or he dies;
Though wondering senates hung on all he spoke,
The club must hail him master of the joke.
Shall parts so various aim at nothing new?
He'll shine a Tully and a Wilmot too.
Then turns repentant, and his God adores
With the same spirit that he drinks and whores;
Enough if all around him but admire,
And now the punk applaud, and now the friar.
Thus with each gift of nature and of art,
And wanting nothing but an honest heart;
Grown all to all, from no one vice exempt;
And most contemptible, to shun contempt;
His passion still to covet general praise,
His life, to forfeit it a thousand ways;
A constant bounty which no friend has made;
An angel tongue, which no man can persuade;
A fool, with more of wit than half mankind,
Too rash for thought, for action too refined;
A tyrant to the wife his heart approves;
A rebel to the very king he loves;
He dies, sad outcast of each church and state,
And, harder still! flagitious, yet not great.
Ask you why Wharton broke through every rule
'Twas all for fear the knaves should call him fool.

Nature well known, no prodigies remain,
Comets are regular, and Wharton plain.

Yet, in this search, the wisest may mistake,
If second qualities for first they take.
When Catiline by rapine swell'd his store;
When Cæsar made a noble dame a whore;
In this the lust, in that the avarice
Were means, not ends; ambition was the vice.
That very Cæsar, born in Scipio's days,
Had aim'd, like him, by chastity at praise.
Lucullus, when frugality could charm,
Had roasted turnips in the Sabine farm.
In vain the observer eyes the builder's toil,
But quite mistakes the scaffold for the pile.

In this one passion man can strength enjoy,
As fits give vigour, just when they destroy.
Time, that on all things lays his lenient hand,
Yet tames not this; it sticks to our last sand.
Consistent in our follies and our sins,
Here honest Nature ends as she begins.

Old politicians chew on wisdom past,
And totter on in business to the last;
As weak, as earnest, and as gravely out,
As sober Lanesborough dancing in the gout.

Behold a reverend sire, whom want of grace
Has made the father of a nameless race,
Shoved from the wall perhaps, or rudely press'd
By his own son, that passes by unbless'd:
Still to his wench he crawls on knocking knees,
And envies every sparrow that he sees.

A salmon's belly, Helluo, was thy fate;
The doctor call'd, declares all help too late:
'Mercy!' cries Helluo, 'mercy on my soul!
Is there no hope? Alas! then bring the jowl.'

The frugal crone, whom praying priests attend,
Still tries to save the hallow'd taper's end,
Collects her breath, as ebbing life retires,
For one puff more, and in that puff expires.

'Odious! in woollen! 'twould a saint provoke,'
(Were the last words that poor Narcissa spoke),
'No, let a charming chintz and Brussels lace
Wrap my cold limbs, and shade my lifeless face:
One would not, sure, be frightful when one's dead—
And, Betty, give this cheek a little red.'

The courtier smooth, who forty years had shined
An humble servant to all human kind,
Just brought out this, when scarce his tongue could stir,
'If—where I'm going—I could serve you, sir?'

'I give and I devise' (old Euclio said,
And sigh'd) 'my lands and tenements to Ned.'
'Your money, sir?' 'My money, sir, what! all?
Why—if I must'—(then wept)—'I give it Paul.'
'The manor, sir?'—'The manor! hold,' (he cried),
'Not that—I cannot part with that'—and died.

And you, brave Cobham! to the latest breath
Shall feel your ruling passion strong in death:
Such in those moments as in all the past,

'Oh, save my country, Heaven!' shall be your last.

EPISTLE II.—TO A LADY.

OF THE CHARACTERS OF WOMEN.

Nothing so true as what you once let fall—
'Most women have no characters at all.'
Matter too soft a lasting mark to bear,
And best distinguish'd by black, brown, or fair.

How many pictures of one nymph we view,
All how unlike each other, all how true!
Arcadia's Countess, here, in ermined pride,
Is there, Pastora by a fountain side.
Here Fannia, leering on her own good man,
And there, a naked Leda with a swan.
Let then the fair one beautifully cry,
In Magdalen's loose hair and lifted eye,
Or dress'd in smiles of sweet Cecilia shine,
With simpering angels, palms, and harps divine;
Whether the charmer sinner it or saint it,
If folly grow romantic, I must paint it.

Come then, the colours and the ground prepare!
Dip in the rainbow, trick her off in air;
Choose a firm cloud, before it fall, and in it
Catch, ere she change, the Cynthia of this minute.

Rufa, whose eye quick glancing o'er the park,
Attracts each light gay meteor of a spark,
Agrees as ill with Rufa studying Locke,
As Sappho's diamonds with her dirty smock;
Or Sappho at her toilet's greasy task,
With Sappho fragrant at an evening mask:
So morning insects that in muck begun,
Shine, buzz, and fly-blow in the setting sun.

How soft is Silia! fearful to offend;
The frail one's advocate, the weak one's friend:
To her, Calista proved her conduct nice;
And good Simplicius asks of her advice.

Sudden, she storms! she raves! You tip the wink,
But spare your censure—Silia does not drink.
All eyes may see from what the change arose,
All eyes may see—a pimple on her nose.

Papillia, wedded to her amorous spark,
Sighs for the shades—'How charming is a park!'
A park is purchased, but the fair he sees
All bathed in tears—'Oh odious, odious trees!'

Ladies, like variegated tulips, show,
'Tis to their changes half their charms we owe;
Fine by defect, and delicately weak,
Their happy spots the nice admirer take.
'Twas thus Calypso once each heart alarm'd,
Awed without virtue, without beauty charm'd;
Her tongue bewitch'd as oddly as her eyes,
Less wit than mimic, more a wit than wise;
Strange graces still, and stranger flights she had,
Was just not ugly, and was just not mad;
Yet ne'er so sure our passion to create,
As when she touch'd the brink of all we hate.

Narcissa's nature, tolerably mild,
To make a wash, would hardly stew a child;
Has even been proved to grant a lover's prayer,
And paid a tradesman once, to make him stare;
Gave alms at Easter, in a Christian trim,
And made a widow happy, for a whim.
Why then declare good-nature is her scorn,
When 'tis by that alone she can be borne
Why pique all mortals, yet affect a name?
A fool to pleasure, yet a slave to fame:
Now deep in Taylor and the Book of Martyrs,
Now drinking citron with his Grace and Chartres:
Now conscience chills her, and now passion burns;
And atheism and religion take their turns;
A very heathen in the carnal part,
Yet still a sad, good Christian at her heart.

See Sin in state, majestically drunk;
Proud as a peeress, prouder as a punk;
Chaste to her husband, frank to all beside,
A teeming mistress, but a barren bride.
What then? let blood and body bear the fault,
Her head's untouch'd, that noble seat of thought:
Such this day's doctrine—in another fit
She sins with poets through pure love of wit.

What has not fired her bosom or her brain—
Cæsar and Tall-boy, Charles and Charlemagne?
As Helluo, late dictator of the feast,
The nose of haut goût, and the tip of taste,
Critiqued your wine, and analysed your meat,
Yet on plain pudding deign'd at home to eat;
So Philomedé, lecturing all mankind
On the soft passion and the taste refined,
The address, the delicacy—stoops at once,
And makes her hearty meal upon a dunce.

Flavia's a wit, has too much sense to pray;
To toast our wants and wishes, is her way;
Nor asks of God, but of her stars, to give
The mighty blessing, 'While we live, to live.'
Then all for death, that opiate of the soul!
Lucretia's dagger, Rosamonda's bowl.
Say, what can cause such impotence of mind?
A spark too fickle, or a spouse too kind.

Wise wretch! with pleasures too refined to please;
With too much spirit to be e'er at ease;
With too much quickness ever to be taught;
With too much thinking to have common thought:
You purchase pain with all that joy can give,
And die of nothing, but a rage to live.

Turn then from wits; and look on Simo's mate,
No ass so meek, no ass so obstinate.
Or her, that owns her faults, but never mends,
Because she's honest, and the best of friends.
Or her, whose life the church and scandal share,
For ever in a passion or a prayer.
Or her, who laughs at hell, but (like her Grace)
Cries, 'Ah! how charming, if there's no such place!'
Or who in sweet vicissitude appears
Of mirth and opium, ratafia and tears,
The daily anodyne, and nightly draught,
To kill those foes to fair ones—time and thought.
Woman and fool are two hard things to hit;
For true no-meaning puzzles more than wit.

But what are these to great Atossa's mind?
Scarce once herself, by turns all womankind!
Who, with herself, or others, from her birth
Finds all her life one warfare upon earth:
Shines, in exposing knaves, and painting fools,
Yet is whate'er she hates and ridicules.

No thought advances, but her eddy brain
Whisks it about, and down it goes again.
Full sixty years the world has been her trade,
The wisest fool much time has ever made.
From loveless youth to uninspected age,
No passion gratified, except her rage.
So much the fury still outran the wit,
The pleasure miss'd her, and the scandal hit.
Who breaks with her, provokes revenge from hell,
But he's a bolder man who dares be well.
Her every turn with violence pursued,
Nor more a storm her hate than gratitude:
To that each passion turns, or soon or late;
Love, if it makes her yield, must make her hate:
Superiors? death! and equals? what a curse!
But an inferior not dependent? worse!
Offend her, and she knows not to forgive:
Oblige her, and she'll hate you while you live:
But die, and she'll adore you—then the bust
And temple rise—then fall again to dust.
Last night, her lord was all that's good and great:
A knave this morning, and his will a cheat.
Strange! by the means defeated of the ends,
By spirit robb'd of power, by warmth of friends,
By wealth of followers! without one distress,
Sick of herself through very selfishness!
Atossa, cursed with every granted prayer,
Childless with all her children, wants an heir.
To heirs unknown descends the unguarded store,
Or wanders, Heaven-directed, to the poor.

Pictures like these, dear Madam, to design,
Asks no firm hand, and no unerring line;
Some wandering touches, some reflected light,
Some flying stroke alone can hit 'em right:
For how should equal colours do the knack?
Chameleons who can paint in white and black?

'Yet Chloe, sure, was form'd without a spot'—
Nature in her then err'd not, but forgot.
'With every pleasing, every prudent part,
Say, what can Chloe want?'—She wants a heart.
She speaks, behaves, and acts just as she ought;
But never, never reach'd one generous thought.
Virtue she finds too painful an endeavour,
Content to dwell in decencies for ever.
So very reasonable, so unmoved,
As never yet to love, or to be loved.

She, while her lover pants upon her breast,
Can mark the figures on an Indian chest;
And when she sees her friend in deep despair,
Observes how much a chintz exceeds mohair.
Forbid it, Heaven! a favour or a debt
She e'er should cancel—but she may forget.
Safe is your secret still in Chloe's ear;
But none of Chloe's shall you ever hear.
Of all her dears she never slander'd one,
But cares not if a thousand are undone.
Would Chloe know if you're alive or dead?
She bids her footman put it in her head.
Chloe is prudent—would you, too, be wise?
Then never break your heart when Chloe dies.

One certain portrait may (I grant) be seen,
Which Heaven has varnish'd out, and made a queen:
The same for ever! and described by all
With truth and goodness, as with crown and ball.
Poets heap virtues, painters gems at will,
And show their zeal, and hide their want of skill.
'Tis well—but, artists! who can paint or write,
To draw the naked is your true delight.
That robe of quality so struts and swells,
None see what parts of nature it conceals:
The exactest traits of body or of mind,
We owe to models of an humble kind.
If Queensberry to strip there's no compelling,
'Tis from a handmaid we must take an Helen
From peer or bishop 'tis no easy thing
To draw the man who loves his God, or king:
Alas! I copy (or my draught would fail)
From honest Mahomet, or plain Parson Hale.

But grant, in public men sometimes are shown,
A woman's seen in private life alone:
Our bolder talents in full light display'd;
Your virtues open fairest in the shade.
Bred to disguise, in public 'tis you hide;
There, none distinguish 'twixt your shame or pride,
Weakness or delicacy; all so nice,
That each may seem a virtue, or a vice.

In men, we various ruling passions find;
In women, two almost divide the kind;
Those, only fix'd, they first or last obey,
The love of pleasure, and the love of sway.

That, Nature gives; and where the lesson taught
Is but to please, can pleasure seem a fault?
Experience, this; by man's oppression curst,
They seek the second not to lose the first.

Men, some to business, some to pleasure take;
But every woman is at heart a rake:
Men, some to quiet, some to public strife;
But every lady would be queen for life.

Yet mark the fate of a whole sex of queens!
Power all their end, but beauty all the means:
In youth they conquer, with so wild a rage,
As leaves them scarce a subject in their age:
For foreign glory, foreign joy, they roam;
No thought of peace or happiness at home.
But wisdom's triumph is well-timed retreat,
As hard a science to the fair as great!
Beauties, like tyrants, old and friendless grown,
Yet hate repose, and dread to be alone,
Worn out in public, weary every eye,
Nor leave one sigh behind them when they die.

Pleasure the sex, as children birds, pursue,
Still out of reach, yet never out of view;
Sure, if they catch, to spoil the toy at most,
To covet flying, and regret when lost:
At last, to follies youth could scarce defend,
It grows their age's prudence to pretend;
Ashamed to own they gave delight before,
Reduced to feign it, when they give no more:
As hags hold Sabbaths, less for joy than spite,
So these their merry, miserable night;
Still round and round the ghosts of beauty glide,
And haunt the places where their honour died.

See how the world its veterans rewards!
A youth of frolics, an old age of cards;
Fair to no purpose, artful to no end,
Young without lovers, old without a friend;
A fop their passion, but their prize a sot,
Alive, ridiculous; and dead, forgot!

Ah, friend! to dazzle let the vain design;
To raise the thought, and touch the heart, be thine!
That charm shall grow, while what fatigues the ring,
Flaunts and goes down, an unregarded thing:
So when the sun's broad beam has tired the sight,

All mild ascends the moon's more sober light,
Serene in virgin modesty she shines,
And unobserved the glaring orb declines.

Oh! bless'd with temper, whose unclouded ray
Can make to-morrow cheerful as to-day;
She, who can love a sister's charms, or hear
Sighs for a daughter with unwounded ear;
She, who ne'er answers till a husband cools,
Or, if she rales him, never shows she rules;
Charms by accepting, by submitting sways,
Yet has her humour most when she obeys;
Let fops or fortune fly which way they will;
Disdains all loss of tickets, or codille;
Spleen, vapours, or small-pox, above them all,
And mistress of herself though China fall.

And yet, believe me, good as well as ill,
Woman's at best a contradiction still.
Heaven, when it strives to polish all it can
Its last, best work, but forms a softer man;
Picks from each sex, to make the favourite blest,
Your love of pleasure or desire of rest:
Blends, in exception to all general rules,
Your taste of follies, with our scorn of fools:
Reserve with frankness, art with truth allied,
Courage with softness, modesty with pride;
Fix'd principles, with fancy ever new;
Shakes all together, and produces—you.

Be this a woman's fame: with this unbless'd,
Toasts live a scorn, and queens may die a jest.
This Phoebus promised (I forget the year)
When those blue eyes first open'd on the sphere;
Ascendant Phoebus watch'd that hour with care,
Averted half your parents' simple prayer;
And gave you beauty, but denied the pelf
That buys your sex a tyrant o'er itself.
The generous god, who wit and gold refines,
And ripens spirits as he ripens mines,
Kept dross for duchesses, the world shall know it,
To you gave sense, good-humour, and a poet.

EPISTLE III.—TO ALLEN LORD BATHURST.

ARGUMENT.

OF THE USE OF RICHES.

That it is known to few, most falling into one of the extremes, avarice or profusion, ver. 1., &c. The point discussed, whether the invention of money has been more commodious, or pernicious to mankind, ver. 21 to 77. That riches, either to the avaricious or the prodigal, cannot afford happiness, scarcely necessaries, ver. 89 to 160. That avarice is an absolute frenzy, without an end or purpose, ver. 113 to 152. Conjectures about the motives of avaricious men, ver. 121 to 153. That the conduct of men, with respect to riches, can only be accounted for by the order of Providence, which works the general good out of extremes, and brings all to its great end by perpetual revolutions, ver. 161 to 178. How a miser acts upon principles which appear to him reasonable, ver. 179. How a prodigal does the same, ver. l99. The due medium, and true use of riches, ver. 219. The Man of Ross, ver. 250. The fate of the profuse and the covetous, in two examples; both miserable in life and in death, ver. 300, &c. The story of Sir Balaam, ver. 339 to the end.

P.
Who shall decide, when doctors disagree,
And soundest casuists doubt, like you and me?
You hold the word, from Jove to Momus given,
That man was made the standing jest of Heaven;
And gold but sent to keep the fools in play,
For some to heap, and some to throw away.

But I, who think more highly of our kind,
(And, surely, Heaven and I are of a mind)
Opine, that Nature, as in duty bound,
Deep hid the shining mischief under ground:
But when, by man's audacious labour won,
Flamed forth this rival to its sire, the Sun,
Then careful Heaven supplied two sorts of men,
To squander these, and those to hide again.

Like doctors thus, when much dispute has pass'd,
We find our tenets just the same at last.
Both fairly owning, riches, in effect,
No grace of Heaven or token of the elect;
Given to the fool, the mad, the vain, the evil,
To Ward, to Waters, Chartres, and the devil.

B.
What nature wants, commodious gold bestows,
'Tis thus we eat the bread another sows.

P.
But how unequal it bestows, observe,
Tis thus we riot, while who sow it starve:
What nature wants (a phrase I much distrust)
Extends to luxury, extends to lust:

Useful, I grant, it serves what life requires,
But dreadful too, the dark assassin hires:

B.
Trade it may help, society extend.

P.
But lures the pirate, and corrupts the friend.

B.
It raises armies in a nation's aid.

P.
But bribes a senate, and the land's betray'd.
In vain may heroes fight, and patriots rave;
If secret gold sap on from knave to knave.
Once, we confess, beneath the patriot's cloak,
From the crack'd bag the dropping guinea spoke,
And jingling down the back-stairs, told the crew,
'Old Cato is as great a rogue as you.'
Blest paper-credit! last and best supply!
That lends corruption lighter wings to fly!
Gold imp'd by thee, can compass hardest things,
Can pocket states, can fetch or carry kings;
A single leaf shall waft an army o'er,
Or ship off senates to a distant shore;
A leaf, like Sibyl's, scatter to and fro
Our fates and fortunes, as the winds shall blow:
Pregnant with thousands flits the scrap unseen,
And silent sells a king, or buys a queen,

Oh! that such bulky bribes as all might see,
Still, as of old, encumber'd villainy!
Could France or Rome divert our brave designs,
With all their brandies, or with all their wines?
What could they more than knights and squires confound,
Or water all the quorum ten miles round?
A statesman's slumbers how this speech would spoil!
'Sir, Spain has sent a thousand jars of oil;
Huge bales of British cloth blockade the door;
A hundred oxen at your leveë roar.'

Poor avarice one torment more would find;
Nor could profusion squander all in kind.
Astride his cheese, Sir Morgan might we meet;
And Worldly crying coals from street to street,
Whom, with a wig so wild, and mien so mazed,
Pity mistakes for some poor tradesman crazed.

Had Colepepper's whole wealth been hops and hogs,
Could he himself have sent it to the dogs?
His Grace will game: to White's a bull be led,
With spurning heels, and with a butting head:
To White's be carried, as to ancient games,
Fair coursers, vases, and alluring dames.
Shall then Uxorio, if the stakes he sweep,
Bear home six whores and make his lady weep?
Or soft Adonis, so perfumed and fine,
Drive to St James's a whole herd of swine?
Oh filthy check on all industrious skill,
To spoil the nation's last great trade—quadrille?
Since then, my lord, on such a world we fall,
What say you?

B.
Say! Why, take it, gold and all.

P.
What riches give us, let us then inquire:
Meat, fire, and clothes.

B.
What more?

P.
Meat, clothes, and fire.
Is this too little? would you more than live?
Alas! 'tis more than Turner finds they give.
Alas! 'tis more than (all his visions past)
Unhappy Wharton, waking, found at last!
What can they give? to dying Hopkins, heirs;
To Chartres, vigour; Japhet, nose and ears?
Can they in gems bid pallid Hippia glow,
In Fulvia's buckle ease the throbs below;
Or heal, old Narses, thy obscener ail,
With all the embroidery plaster'd at thy tail?
They might (were Harpax not too wise to spend)
Give Harpax' self the blessing of a friend;
Or find some doctor that would save the life
Of wretched Shylock, spite of Shylock's wife:
But thousands die, without or this or that,
Die, and endow a college, or a cat.
To some, indeed, Heaven grants the happier fate,
T' enrich a bastard, or a son they hate.

Perhaps you think the poor might have their part?
Bond damns the poor, and hates them from his heart:

The grave Sir Gilbert holds it for a rule,
That 'every man in want is knave or fool:'
'God cannot love' (says Blunt, with tearless eyes)
'The wretch he starves'—and piously denies:
But the good bishop, with a meeker air,
Admits, and leaves them, Providence's care.

Yet, to be just to these poor men of pelf,
Each does but hate his neighbour as himself:
Damn'd to the mines, an equal fate betides
The slave that digs it, and the slave that hides.

B.
Who suffer thus, mere charity should own,
Must act on motives powerful, though unknown.

P.
Some war, some plague, or famine, they foresee,
Some revelation hid from you and me.
Why Shylock wants a meal, the cause is found,
He thinks a loaf will rise to fifty pound.
What made directors cheat in South-sea year?
To live on venison when it sold so dear.
Ask you why Phryne the whole auction buys?
Phryne foresees a general excise.
Why she and Sappho raise that monstrous sum?
Alas! they fear a man will cost a plum.

Wise Peter sees the world's respect for gold,
And therefore hopes this nation may be sold:
Glorious ambition! Peter, swell thy store,
And be what Rome's great Didius was before.

The crown of Poland, venal twice an age,
To just three millions stinted modest Gage.
But nobler scenes Maria's dreams unfold,
Hereditary realms, and worlds of gold.
Congenial souls! whose life one avarice joins,
And one fate buries in the Asturian mines.

Much-injured Blunt! why bears he Britain's hate?
A wizard told him in these words our fate:
'At length corruption, like a general flood,
(So long by watchful ministers withstood)
Shall deluge all; and avarice creeping on,
Spread like a low-born mist, and blot the sun,
Statesman and patriot ply alike the stocks,
Peeress and butler share alike the box,

And judges job, and bishops bite the town,
And mighty dukes pack cards for half-a-crown.
See Britain sunk in lucre's sordid charms,
And France revenged of Anne's and Edward's arms!'
'Twas no court-badge, great scrivener! fired thy brain,
Nor lordly luxury, nor city gain:
No, 'twas thy righteous end, ashamed to see
Senates degenerate, patriots disagree,
And nobly wishing party-rage to cease,
To buy both sides, and give thy country peace.

'All this is madness,' cries a sober sage:
But who, my friend, has reason in his rage?
'The ruling passion, be it what it will,
The ruling passion conquers reason still.'
Less mad the wildest whimsy we can frame,
Than even that passion, if it has no aim;
For though such motives folly you may call,
The folly's greater to have none at all.

Hear, then, the truth: ''Tis Heaven each passion sends,
And different men directs to different ends.
Extremes in Nature equal good produce,
Extremes in man concur to general use.'
Ask we what makes one keep, and one bestow?
That Power who bids the ocean ebb and flow,
Bids seed-time, harvest, equal course maintain,
Through reconciled extremes of drought and rain.
Builds life on death, on change duration founds,
And gives the eternal wheels to know their rounds.

Riches, like insects, when conceal'd they lie,
Wait but for wings, and in their season fly.
Who sees pale Mammon pine amidst his store,
Sees but a backward steward for the poor;
This year a reservoir, to keep and spare,
The next a fountain, spouting through his heir,
In lavish streams to quench a country's thirst,
And men and dogs shall drink him till they burst.

Old Cotta shamed his fortune and his birth,
Yet was not Cotta void of wit or worth:
What though (the use of barbarous spits forgot)
His kitchen vied in coolness with his grot?
His court with nettles, moats with cresses stored,
With soups unbought and salads bless'd his board?
If Cotta lived on pulse, it was no more
Than Brahmins, saints, and sages did before;

To cram the rich was prodigal expense,
And who would take the poor from Providence?
Like some lone Chartreux stands the good old Hall,
Silence without, and fasts within the wall;
No rafter'd roofs with dance and tabor sound,
No noontide-bell invites the country round:
Tenants with sighs the smokeless towers survey,
And turn the unwilling steeds another way:
Benighted wanderers, the forest o'er,
Curse the saved candle, and unopening door;
While the gaunt mastiff growling at the gate,
Affrights the beggar whom he longs to eat.

Not so his son; he mark'd this oversight,
And then mistook reverse of wrong for right.
(For what to shun will no great knowledge need,
But what to follow, is a task indeed).
Yet sure, of qualities deserving praise,
More go to ruin fortunes, than to raise.
What slaughter'd hecatombs, what floods of wine,
Fill the capacious squire, and deep divine!
Yet no mean motive this profusion draws,
His oxen perish in his country's cause;
'Tis George and Liberty that crowns the cup,
And zeal for that great house which eats him up.
The woods recede around the naked seat,
The silvans groan—no matter—for the fleet;
Next goes his wool—to clothe our valiant bands,
Last, for his country's love, he sells his lands.
To town he comes, completes the nation's hope,
And heads the bold train-bands, and burns a pope.
And shall not Britain now reward his toils,
Britain, that pays her patriots with her spoils?
In vain at court the bankrupt pleads his cause,
His thankless country leaves him to her laws.

The sense to value riches, with the art
To enjoy them, and the virtue to impart,
Not meanly, nor ambitiously pursued,
Not sunk by sloth, nor raised by servitude:
To balance fortune by a just expense,
Join with economy, magnificence;
With splendour, charity; with plenty, health;
Oh teach us, Bathurst! yet unspoil'd by wealth!
That secret rare, between the extremes to move
Of mad good-nature and of mean self-love.

B.

To worth or want well-weigh'd, be bounty given,
And ease, or emulate, the care of Heaven;
(Whose measure full o'erflows on human race)
Mend Fortune's fault, and justify her grace.
Wealth in the gross is death, but life, diffused;
As poison heals, in just proportion used:
In heaps, like ambergris, a stink it lies,
But well-dispersed, is incense to the skies.

P.

Who starves by nobles, or with nobles eats?
The wretch that trusts them, and the rogue that cheats.
Is there a lord, who knows a cheerful noon
Without a fiddler, flatterer, or buffoon?
Whose table, wit, or modest merit share,
Unelbow'd by a gamester, pimp, or player?
Who copies yours, or Oxford's better part,
To ease the oppress'd, and raise the sinking heart?
Where'er he shines, O Fortune! gild the scene,
And angels guard him in the golden mean!
There, English bounty yet awhile may stand,
And honour linger ere it leaves the land.

But all our praises why should lords engross?
Rise, honest Muse! and sing the Man of Ross:
Pleased Vaga echoes through her winding bounds,
And rapid Severn hoarse applause resounds.
Who hung with woods yon mountain's sultry brow?
From the dry rock who bade the waters flow?
Not to the skies in useless columns toss'd,
Or in proud falls magnificently lost,
But clear and artless pouring through the plain
Health to the sick, and solace to the swain.
Whose causeway parts the vale with shady rows?
Whose seats the weary traveller repose?
Who taught that heaven-directed spire to rise?
'The Man of Ross,' each lisping babe replies.
Behold the market-place with poor o'erspread!
The Man of Ross divides the weekly bread:
He feeds yon alms-house, neat, but void of state,
Where Age and Want sit smiling at the gate:
Him portion'd maids, apprenticed orphans bless'd,
The young who labour, and the old who rest.
Is any sick? the Man of Ross relieves,
Prescribes, attends, the medicine makes, and gives.
Is there a variance? enter but his door,
Balk'd are the courts, and contest is no more.
Despairing quacks with curses fled the place,

And vile attorneys, now a useless race.

B.
Thrice happy man! enabled to pursue
What all so wish, but want the power to do!
Oh say, what sums that generous hand supply?
What mines, to swell that boundless charity?

P.
Of debts and taxes, wife and children clear,
This man possess'd—five hundred pounds a-year.
Blush, Grandeur, blush! proud courts, withdraw your blaze!
Ye little stars, hide your diminish'd rays!

B.
And what? no monument, inscription, stone?
His race, his form, his name almost unknown?

P.
Who builds a church to God, and not to fame,
Will never mark the marble with his name:
Go, search it there, where to be born and die,
Of rich and poor makes all the history;
Enough, that virtue fill'd the space between;
Proved, by the ends of being, to have been.
When Hopkins dies, a thousand lights attend
The wretch who, living, saved a candle's end:
Shouldering God's altar a vile image stands,
Belies his features, nay, extends his hands;
That live-long wig which Gorgon's self might own,
Eternal buckle takes in Parian stone.
Behold what blessings wealth to life can lend!
And see what comfort it affords our end!

In the worst inn's worst room, with mat half-hung,
The floors of plaster, and the walls of dung,
On once a flock-bed, but repair'd with straw,
With tape-tied curtains, never meant to draw,
The George and Garter dangling from that bed
Where tawdry yellow strove with dirty red,
Great Villiers lies—alas! how changed from him,
That life of pleasure, and that soul of whim!
Gallant and gay, in Cliveden's proud alcove,
The bower of wanton Shrewsbury, and love;
Or just as gay, at council, in a ring
Of mimick'd statesmen, and their merry king.
No wit to flatter, left of all his store;
No fool to laugh at, which he valued more.

There, victor of his health, of fortune, friends,
And fame, this lord of useless thousands ends.

His Grace's fate sage Cutler could foresee,
And well (he thought) advised him, 'Live like me.'
As well his Grace replied, 'Like you, Sir John?
That I can do, when all I have is gone.'
Resolve me, Reason, which of these is worse,
Want with a full, or with an empty purse?
Thy life more wretched, Cutler, was confess'd,
Arise, and tell me, was thy death more bless'd?
Cutler saw tenants break, and houses fall;
For very want he could not build a wall.
His only daughter in a stranger's power;
For very want he could not pay a dower.
A few gray hairs his reverend temples crown'd,
'Twas very want that sold them for two pound.
What even denied a cordial at his end,
Banish'd the doctor, and expell'd the friend?
What but a want, which you perhaps think mad,
Yet numbers feel—the want of what he had!
Cutler and Brutus, dying, both exclaim,
'Virtue! and Wealth! what are ye but a name!'

Say, for such worth are other worlds prepared
Or are they both in this their own reward?
A knotty point! to which we now proceed.
But you are tired—I'll tell a tale—

B.
Agreed.

P.
Where London's column, pointing at the skies
Like a tall bully, lifts the head, and lies;
There dwelt a citizen of sober fame,
A plain good man, and Balaam was his name;
Religious, punctual, frugal, and so forth;
His word would pass for more than he was worth.
One solid dish his week-day meal affords,
An added pudding solemnised the Lord's:
Constant at church, and 'Change; his gains were sure,
His givings rare, save farthings to the poor.

The devil was piqued such saintship to behold,
And long'd to tempt him like good Job of old:
But Satan now is wiser than of yore,
And tempts by making rich, not making poor.

Roused by the Prince of Air, the whirlwinds sweep
The surge, and plunge his father in the deep;
Then lull against his Cornish lands they roar,
And two rich shipwrecks bless the lucky shore.

Sir Balaam now, he lives like other folks,
He takes his chirping pint, and cracks his jokes:
'Live like yourself,' was soon my Lady's word;
And, lo! two puddings smoked upon the board.

Asleep and naked as an Indian lay,
An honest factor stole a gem away:
He pledged it to the knight; the knight had wit,
So kept the diamond, and the rogue was bit.
Some scruple rose, but thus he eased his thought—
'I'll now give sixpence where I gave a groat;
Where once I went to church, I'll now go twice—
And am so clear, too, of all other vice.'

The Tempter saw his time; the work he plied;
Stocks and subscriptions pour on every side,
Till all the demon makes his full descent
In one abundant shower of cent, per cent.;
Sinks deep within him, and possesses whole,
Then dubs director, and secures his soul.

Behold Sir Balaam, now a man of spirit,
Ascribes his gettings to his parts and merit;
What late he call'd a blessing, now was wit,
And God's good providence, a lucky hit.
Things change their titles, as our manners turn:
His counting-house employ'd the Sunday-morn;
Seldom at church ('twas such a busy life)
But duly sent his family and wife.
There (so the devil ordain'd) one Christmas-tide,
My good old lady catch'd a cold, and died.

A nymph of quality admires our knight;
He marries, bows at court, and grows polite:
Leaves the dull cits, and joins (to please the fair)
The well-bred cuckolds in St James's air:
First, for his son a gay commission buys,
Who drinks, whores, fights, and in a duel dies:
His daughter flaunts a viscount's tawdry wife;
She bears a coronet and pox for life.
In Britain's senate he a seat obtains,
And one more pensioner St Stephen gains.

My lady falls to play; so bad her chance,
He must repair it; takes a bribe from France;
The House impeach him; Coningsby harangues;
The court forsake him—and Sir Balaam hangs:
Wife, son, and daughter, Satan! are thy own,
His wealth, yet dearer, forfeit to the crown:
The devil and the king divide the prize,
And sad Sir Balaam curses God, and dies.

EPISTLE IV.—TO RICHARD BOYLE, EARL OF BURLINGTON.

ARGUMENT.

OF THE USE OF RICHES.

The vanity of expense in people of wealth and quality. The abuse of the word 'taste,' ver. 13. That the
first principle and foundation, in this as in every thing else, is good sense, ver. 40. The chief proof of it is
to follow nature, even in works of mere luxury and elegance. Instanced in architecture and gardening,
where all must be adapted to the genius and use of the place, and the beauties not forced into it, but
resulting from it, ver. 50. How men are disappointed in their most expensive undertakings, for want of
this true foundation, without which nothing can please long, if at all; and the best examples and rules
will but be perverted into something burdensome or ridiculous, ver. 65 to 92. A description of the false
taste of magnificence; the first grand error of which is to imagine that greatness consists in the size and
dimension, instead of the proportion and harmony of the whole, ver. 97; and the second, either in
joining together parts incoherent, or too minutely resembling, or in the repetition of the same too
frequently, ver. 105, &c. A word or two of false taste in books, in music, in painting, even in preaching
and prayer, and lastly in entertainments, ver. 133, &c. Yet Providence is justified in giving wealth to be
squandered in this manner, since it is dispersed to the poor and laborious part of mankind, ver. 169
[recurring to what is laid down in the 'Essay on Man,' ep. ii. and in the epistle preceding this, ver. 159,
&c.] What are the proper objects of magnificence, and a proper field for the expense of great men, ver.
177, &c.; and finally, the great and public works which become a prince, ver. 191, to the end.

'Tis strange, the miser should his cares employ
To gain those riches he can ne'er enjoy:
Is it less strange, the prodigal should waste
His wealth, to purchase what he ne'er can taste?
Not for himself he sees, or hears, or eats;
Artists must choose his pictures, music, meats;
He buys for Topham drawings and designs,
For Pembroke statues, dirty gods, and coins;
Rare monkish manuscripts for Hearne alone,
And books for Mead, and butterflies for Sloane.
Think we all these are for himself? no more
Than his fine wife, alas! or finer whore.

For what has Virro painted, built, and planted?
Only to show how many tastes he wanted.
What brought Sir Visto's ill-got wealth to waste?
Some demon whisper'd, 'Visto! have a taste.'
Heaven visits with a taste the wealthy fool,
And needs no rod but Ripley with a rule.
See! sportive fate, to punish awkward pride,
Bids Bubo build, and sends him such a guide:
A standing sermon, at each year's expense,
That never coxcomb reach'd magnificence!

You show us, Rome was glorious, not profuse,
And pompous buildings once were things of use.
Yet shall (my lord) your just, your noble rules
Fill half the land with imitating fools,
Who random drawings from your sheets shall take,
And of one beauty many blunders make;
Load some vain church with old theatric state,
Turn arcs of triumph to a garden-gate;
Reverse your ornaments, and hang them all
On some patch'd dog-hole eked with ends of wall;
Then clap four slices of pilaster on't,
That, laced with bits of rustic, makes a front.
Shall call the winds through long arcades to roar,
Proud to catch cold at a Venetian door;
Conscious they act a true Palladian part.
And if they starve, they starve by rules of art.

Oft have you hinted to your brother peer,
A certain truth, which many buy too dear:
Something there is more needful than expense,
And something previous even to taste—'tis sense:
Good sense, which only is the gift of Heaven,
And though no science, fairly worth the seven:
A light, which in yourself you must perceive;
Jones and Le Nôtre have it not to give.

To build, to plant, whatever you intend,
To rear the column, or the arch to bend,
To swell the terrace, or to sink the grot;
In all, let Nature never be forgot.
But treat the goddess like a modest fair,
Nor overdress, nor leave her wholly bare;
Let not each beauty everywhere be spied,
Where half the skill is decently to hide.
He gains all points, who pleasingly confounds,
Surprises, varies, and conceals the bounds.

Consult the genius of the place in all;
That tells the waters or to rise, or fall;
Or helps the ambitious hill the heavens to scale,
Or scoops in circling theatres the vale;
Calls in the country, catches opening glades,
Joins willing woods, and varies shades from shades;
Now breaks, or now directs, the intending lines;
Paints as you plant, and, as you work, designs.

Still follow sense, of every art the soul,
Parts answering parts shall slide into a whole,
Spontaneous beauties all around advance,
Start even from difficulty, strike from chance;
Nature shall join you; time shall make it grow
A work to wonder at—perhaps a Stowe.

Without it, proud Versailles! thy glory falls;
And Nero's terraces desert their walls:
The vast parterres a thousand hands shall make,
Lo! Cobham comes, and floats them with a lake:
Or cut wide views through mountains to the plain,
You'll wish your hill or shelter'd seat again.
Even in an ornament its place remark,
Nor in an hermitage set Dr Clarke.
Behold Villario's ten years' toil complete;
His quincunx darkens, his espaliers meet;
The wood supports the plain, the parts unite,
And strength of shade contends with strength of light;
A waving glow the blooming beds display,
Blushing in bright diversities of day,
With silver-quivering rills meander'd o'er—
Enjoy them, you! Villario can no more;
Tired of the scene parterres and fountains yield,
He finds at last he better likes a field.

Through his young woods how pleased Sabinus stray'd,
Or sat delighted in the thickening shade,
With annual joy the reddening shoots to greet,
Or see the stretching branches long to meet!
His son's fine taste an opener vista loves,
Foe to the Dryads of his father's groves;
One boundless green, or flourish'd carpet views,
With all the mournful family of yews;
The thriving plants, ignoble broomsticks made,
Now sweep those alleys they were born to shade.

At Timon's villa let us pass a day,
Where all cry out, 'What sums are thrown away!'

So proud, so grand; of that stupendous air,
Soft and agreeable come never there.
Greatness, with Timon, dwells in such a draught
As brings all Brobdignag before your thought.
To compass this, his building is a town,
His pond an ocean, his parterre a down:
Who but must laugh, the master when he sees,
A puny insect, shivering at a breeze!
Lo, what huge heaps of littleness around!
The whole a labour'd quarry above ground;
Two Cupids squirt before: a lake behind
Improves the keenness of the northern wind.
His gardens next your admiration call,
On every side you look, behold the wall!
No pleasing intricacies intervene,
No artful wildness to perplex the scene;
Grove nods at grove, each alley has a brother,
And half the platform just reflects the other.
The suffering eye inverted nature sees,
Trees cut to statues, statues thick as trees;
With here a fountain, never to be play'd;
And there a summer-house, that knows no shade;
Here Amphitritè sails through myrtle bowers;
There gladiators fight, or die in flowers;
Unwater'd see the drooping sea-horse mourn,
And swallows roost in Nilus' dusty urn.

My lord advances with majestic mien,
Smit with the mighty pleasure, to be seen:
But soft—by regular approach—not yet—
First through the length of yon hot terrace sweat;
And when up ten steep slopes you've dragg'd your thighs,
Just at his study-door he'll bless your eyes.

His study! with what authors is it stored?
In books, not authors, curious is my lord;
To all their dated backs he turns you round:
These Aldus printed, those Du Sueil has bound.
Lo! some are vellum, and the rest as good
For all his lordship knows, but they are wood.
For Locke or Milton 'tis in vain to look,
These shelves admit not any modern book.

And now the chapel's silver bell you hear,
That summons you to all the pride of prayer:
Light quirks of music, broken and uneven,
Make the soul dance upon a jig to heaven.
On painted ceilings you devoutly stare,

Where sprawl the saints of Verrio or Laguerre,
On gilded clouds in fair expansion lie,
And bring all Paradise before your eye.
To rest, the cushion and soft dean invite,
Who never mentions hell to ears polite.

But hark! the chiming clocks to dinner call;
A hundred footsteps scrape the marble hall:
The rich buffet well-colour'd serpents grace,
And gaping Tritons spew to wash your face.
Is this a dinner? this a genial room?
No, 'tis a temple, and a hecatomb.
A solemn sacrifice, perform'd in state,
You drink by measure, and to minutes eat.
So quick retires each flying course, you'd swear
Sancho's dread doctor and his wand were there.
Between each act the trembling salvers ring,
From soup to sweet-vine, and God bless the king.
In plenty starving, tantalised in state,
And complaisantly help'd to all I hate,
Treated, caress'd, and tired, I take my leave,
Sick of his civil pride from morn to eve;
I curse such lavish cost, and little skill,
And swear no day was ever pass'd so ill.

Yet hence the poor are clothed, the hungry fed;
Health to himself, and to his infants bread
The labourer bears: what his hard heart denies,
His charitable vanity supplies.

Another age shall see the golden ear
Imbrown the slope, and nod on the parterre,
Deep harvests bury all his pride has plann'd,
And laughing Ceres reassume the land.

Who then shall grace, or who improve the soil?—
Who plants like Bathurst, or who builds like Boyle.
'Tis use alone that sanctifies expense,
And splendour borrows all her rays from sense.

His father's acres who enjoys in peace,
Or makes his neighbours glad, if he increase:
Whose cheerful tenants bless their yearly toil,
Yet to their lord owe more than to the soil;
Whose ample lawns are not ashamed to feed
The milky heifer and deserving steed;
Whose rising forests, not for pride or show,
But future buildings, future navies, grow:

Let his plantations stretch from down to down,
First shade a country, and then raise a town.

You, too, proceed! make falling arts your care,
Erect new wonders, and the old repair;
Jones and Palladio to themselves restore,
And be whate'er Vitruvius was before:
Till kings call forth the ideas of your mind,
(Proud to accomplish what such hands design'd.)
Bid harbours open, public ways extend,
Bid temples, worthier of the god, ascend;
Bid the broad arch the dangerous flood contain,
The mole projected break the roaring main;
Back to his bonds their subject sea command,
And roll obedient rivers through the land;
These honours, peace to happy Britain brings,
These are imperial works, and worthy kings.

EPISTLE V. TO MR ADDISON.

OCCASIONED BY HIS DIALOGUES ON MEDALS.

See the wild waste of all-devouring years!
How Rome her own sad sepulchre appears,
With nodding arches, broken temples spread!
The very tombs now vanish'd, like their dead!
Imperial wonders raised on nations spoil'd
Where mix'd with slaves the groaning martyr toil'd:
Huge theatres, that now unpeopled woods,
Now drain'd a distant country of her floods:
Fanes, which admiring gods with pride survey,
Statues of men, scarce less alive than they!
Some felt the silent stroke of mouldering age,
Some hostile fury, some religious rage,
Barbarian blindness, Christian zeal conspire,
And Papal piety, and Gothic fire.
Perhaps, by its own ruins saved from flame,
Some buried marble half-preserves a name;
That name the learn'd with fierce disputes pursue,
And give to Titus old Vespasian's due.

Ambition sigh'd: she found it vain to trust
The faithless column, and the crumbling bust:
Huge moles, whose shadow stretch'd from shore to shore,
Their ruins perish'd, and their place no more!
Convinced, she now contracts her vast design,

And all her triumphs shrink into a coin.
A narrow orb each crowded conquest keeps,
Beneath her palm, here sad Judæa weeps.
Now scantier limits the proud arch confine,
And scarce are seen the prostrate Nile or Rhine;
A small Euphrates through the piece is roll'd,
And little eagles wave their wings in gold.

The medal, faithful to its charge of fame,
Through climes and ages bears each form and name:
In one short view subjected to our eye
Gods, emperors, heroes, sages, beauties, lie.
With sharpen'd sight, pale antiquaries pore,
The inscription value, but the rust adore.
This the blue varnish, that the green endears,
The sacred rust of twice ten hundred years!
To gain Pescennius one employs his schemes,
One grasps a Cecrops in ecstatic dreams.
Poor Vadius, long with learned spleen devour'd.
Can taste no pleasure since his shield was scour'd:
And Curio, restless by the fair one's side,
Sighs for an Otho, and neglects his bride.

Theirs is the vanity, the learning thine:
Touch'd by thy hand, again Rome's glories shine;
Her gods, and god-like heroes rise to view,
And all her faded garlands bloom anew.
Nor blush, these studies thy regard engage;
These pleased the fathers of poetic rage;
The verse and sculpture bore an equal part,
And Art reflected images to Art.

Oh! when shall Britain, conscious of her claim,
Stand emulous of Greek and Roman fame?
In living medals see her wars enroll'd,
And vanquish'd realms supply recording gold?
Here, rising bold, the patriot's honest face;
There, warriors frowning in historic brass:
Then future ages with delight shall see
How Plato's, Bacon's, Newton's looks agree;
Or in fair series laurell'd bards be shown,
A Virgil there, and here an Addison.
Then shall thy Craggs (and let me call him mine)
On the cast ore, another Pollio, shine;
With aspect open, shall erect his head,
And round the orb in lasting notes be read,
'Statesman, yet friend to truth! of soul sincere,
In action faithful, and in honour clear;

Who broke no promise, served no private end,
Who gain'd no title, and who lost no friend;
Ennobled by himself, by all approved,
And praised, unenvied, by the Muse he loved.'

A PROLOGUE

TO A PLAY FOR MR DENNIS'S BENEFIT, IN 1733, WHEN HE WAS OLD, BLIND, AND IN GREAT DISTRESS,
A LITTLE BEFORE HIS DEATH.

As when that hero, who, in each campaign,
Had braved the Goth, and many a Vandal slain,
Lay fortune-struck, a spectacle of woe!
Wept by each friend, forgiven by every foe:
Was there a generous, a reflecting mind,
But pitied Belisarius, old and blind?
Was there a chief but melted at the sight?
A common soldier, but who clubb'd his mite?
Such, such emotions should in Britons rise,
When press'd by want and weakness Dennis lies;
Dennis, who long had warr'd with modern Huns,
Their quibbles routed, and defied their puns;
A desperate bulwark, sturdy, firm, and fierce,
Against the Gothic sons of frozen verse:
How changed from him who made the boxes groan,
And shook the stage with thunders all his own!
Stood up to dash each vain pretender's hope,
Maul the French tyrant, or pull down the Pope!
If there's a Briton then, true bred and born,
Who holds dragoons and wooden shoes in scorn;
If there's a critic of distinguished rage;
If there's a senior who contemns this age:
Let him to night his just assistance lend,
And be the critic's, Briton's, old man's friend.

PROLOGUE TO MR ADDISON'S 'CATO.'

To wake the soul by tender strokes of art,
To raise the genius, and to mend the heart;
To make mankind, in conscious virtue bold,
Live o'er each scene, and be what they behold:
For this the tragic Muse first trod the stage,

Commanding tears to stream through every age;
Tyrants no more their savage nature kept,
And foes to virtue wonder'd how they wept.
Our author shuns by vulgar springs to move
The hero's glory, or the virgin's love;
In pitying love, we but our weakness show,
And wild ambition well deserves its woe.
Here tears shall flow from a more generous cause,
Such tears as patriots shed for dying laws:
He bids your breasts with ancient ardour rise,
And calls forth Roman drops from British eyes.
Virtue confess'd in human shape he draws,
What Plato thought, and godlike Cato was:
No common object to your sight displays,
But what with pleasure Heaven itself surveys,
A brave man struggling in the storms of fate,
And greatly falling with a falling state.
While Cato gives his little senate laws,
What bosom beats not in his country's cause?
Who sees him act, but envies every deed?
Who hears him groan, and does not wish to bleed?
E'en when proud Caesar, 'midst triumphal cars,
The spoils of nations, and the pomp of wars,
Ignobly vain, and impotently great,
Show'd Rome her Cato's figure drawn in state;
As her dead father's reverend image pass'd,
The pomp was darkened, and the day o'ercast;
The triumph ceased, tears gush'd from every eye;
The world's great victor pass'd unheeded by;
Her last good man dejected Rome adored,
And honour'd Caesar's less than Cato's sword.

Britons, attend: be worth like this approved,
And show you have the virtue to be moved.
With honest scorn the first famed Cato view'd
Rome learning arts from Greece, whom she subdued:
Your scene precariously subsists too long
On French translation and Italian song.
Dare to have sense yourselves; assert the stage,
Be justly warm'd with your own native rage:
Such plays alone should win a British ear,
As Cato's self had not disdain'd to hear.

PROLOGUE TO THOMSON'S 'SOPHONISBA.'

When Learning, after the long Gothic night,

Fair, o'er the western world, renew'd its light,
With arts arising, Sophonisba rose;
The tragic Muse, returning, wept her woes.
With her th' Italian scene first learn'd to glow,
And the first tears for her were taught to flow:
Her charms the Gallic Muses next inspired;
Corneille himself saw, wonder'd, and was fired.

What foreign theatres with pride have shown,
Britain, by juster title, makes her own.
When freedom is the cause, 'tis hers to fight,
And hers, when freedom is the theme, to write.
For this a British author bids again
The heroine rise, to grace the British scene:
Here, as in life, she breathes her genuine flame,
She asks, What bosom has not felt the same?
Asks of the British youth—is silence there?
She dares to ask it of the British fair.
To-night our homespun author would be true,
At once to nature, history, and you.
Well pleased to give our neighbours due applause,
He owns their learning, but disdains their laws;
Not to his patient touch, or happy flame,
'Tis to his British heart he trusts for fame.
If France excel him in one freeborn thought,
The man, as well as poet, is in fault.
Nature! informer of the poet's art,
Whose force alone can raise or melt the heart,
Thou art his guide; each passion, every line,
Whate'er he draws to please, must all be thine.
Be thou his judge: in every candid breast
Thy silent whisper is the sacred test.

PROLOGUE, DESIGNED FOR MR D'URFEY'S LAST PLAY.

Grown old in rhyme, 'twere barbarous to discard
Your persevering, unexhausted bard;
Damnation follows death in other men,
But your damn'd poet lives and writes again.
The adventurous lover is successful still,
Who strives to please the fair against her will:
Be kind, and make him in his wishes easy,
Who in your own despite has strove to please ye.
He scorn'd to borrow from the wits of yore,
But ever writ, as none e'er writ before.
You modern wits, should each man bring his claim,

Have desperate debentures on your fame;
And little would be left you, I'm afraid,
If all your debts to Greece and Rome were paid.
From this deep fund our author largely draws,
Nor sinks his credit lower than it was.
Though plays for honour in old time he made,
'Tis now for better reasons—to be paid.
Believe him, he has known the world too long,
And seen the death of much immortal song.
He says, poor poets lost, while players won,
As pimps grow rich, while gallants are undone.
Though Tom the poet writ with ease and pleasure,
The comic Tom abounds in other treasure.
Fame is at best an unperforming cheat;
But 'tis substantial happiness to eat.
Let ease, his last request, be of your giving,
Nor force him to be damn'd to get his living.

PROLOGUE TO 'THE THREE HOURS AFTER MARRIAGE'

Authors are judged by strange capricious rules;
The great ones are thought mad, the small ones fools:
Yet sure the best are most severely fated;
For fools are only laugh'd at, wits are hated.
Blockheads with reason men of sense abhor;
But fool 'gainst fool, is barbarous civil war.
Why on all authors, then, should critics fall?
Since some have writ, and shown no wit at all.
Condemn a play of theirs, and they evade it;
Cry, 'Damn not us, but damn the French, who made it.'
By running goods these graceless owlers gain;
Theirs are the rules of France, the plots of Spain;
But wit, like wine, from happier climates brought,
Dash'd by these rogues, turns English common draught.
They pall Molière's and Lopez' sprightly strain,
And teach dull harlequins to grin in vain.

How shall our author hope a gentler fate,
Who dares most impudently not translate?
It had been civil, in these ticklish times,
To fetch his fools and knaves from foreign climes;
Spaniards and French abuse to the world's end,
But spare old England, lest you hurt a friend.
If any fool is by our satire bit,
Let him hiss loud, to show you all he's hit.
Poets make characters, as salesmen clothes;

We take no measure of your fops and beaux;
But here all sizes and all shapes you meet,
And fit yourselves, like chaps in Monmouth Street.

Gallants, look here! this fool's cap has an air,
Goodly and smart, with ears of Issachar.
Let no one fool engross it, or confine
A common blessing: now 'tis yours, now mine.
But poets in all ages had the care
To keep this cap for such as will, to wear.
Our author has it now (for every wit
Of course resign'd it to the next that writ)
And thus upon the stage 'tis fairly thrown;
Let him that takes it wear it as his own.

EPILOGUE TO MR ROWE'S 'JANE SHORE.'

DESIGNED FOR MRS OLDFIELD.

Prodigious this! the frail one of our play
From her own sex should mercy find to-day!
You might have held the pretty head aside,
Peep'd in your fans, been serious thus, and cried—
'The play may pass—but that strange creature, Shore,
I can't—indeed now—I so hate a whore—'
Just as a blockhead rubs his thoughtless skull,
And thanks his stars he was not born a fool;
So from a sister sinner you shall hear,
'How strangely you expose yourself, my dear!'
But let me die, all raillery apart,
Our sex are still forgiving at their heart;
And, did not wicked custom so contrive,
We'd be the best good-natured things alive.

There are, 'tis true, who tell another tale,
That virtuous ladies envy while they rail;
Such rage without, betrays the fire within;
In some close corner of the soul they sin;
Still hoarding up, most scandalously nice,
Amidst their virtues a reserve of vice.
The godly dame, who fleshly failings damns,
Scolds with her maid, or with her chaplain crams.
Would you enjoy soft nights and solid dinners?
Faith, gallants, board with saints, and bed with sinners,

Well, if our author in the wife offends,

He has a husband that will make amends;
He draws him gentle, tender, and forgiving;
And sure such kind good creatures may be living.
In days of old, they pardon'd breach of vows,
Stern Cato's self was no relentless spouse:
Plu—Plutarch, what's his name that writes his life?
Tells us, that Cato dearly loved his wife:
Yet if a friend, a night or so, should need her,
He'd recommend her as a special breeder.
To lend a wife, few here would scruple make;
But, pray, which of you all would take her back?
Though with the Stoic chief our stage may ring,
The Stoic husband was the glorious thing.
The man had courage, was a sage, 'tis true,
And loved his country—but what's that to you?
Those strange examples ne'er were made to fit ye,
But the kind cuckold might instruct the city:
There, many an honest man may copy Cato,
Who ne'er saw naked sword, or look'd in Plato.

If, after all, you think it a disgrace,
That Edward's miss thus perks it in your face;
To see a piece of failing flesh and blood,
In all the rest so impudently good;
Faith, let the modest matrons of the town
Come here in crowds, and stare the strumpet down.

Alexander Pope – A Short Biography

Alexander Pope was born in Lombard Street, London, on the 21st of May 1688—the year of the Revolution. His father was a linen-merchant, in thriving circumstances, and said to have noble blood in his veins. His mother was Edith or Editha Turner, daughter of William Turner, Esq., of York. Mr Carruthers, in his excellent Life of the Poet, mentions that there was an Alexander Pope, a clergyman, in the remote parish of Reay, in Caithness, who rode all the way to Twickenham to pay his great namesake a visit, and was presented by him with a copy of the subscription edition of the "Odyssey," in five volumes quarto, which is still preserved by his descendants. Pope's father had made about £10,000 by trade; but being a Roman Catholic, and fond of a country life, he retired from business shortly after the Revolution, at the early age of forty-six. He resided first at Kensington, and then in Binfield, in the neighbourhood of Windsor Forest. He is said to have put his money in a strong box, and to have lived on the principal. His great delight was in his garden; and both he and his wife seem to have cherished the warmest interest in their son, who was very delicate in health, and their only child. Pope's study is still preserved in Binfield; and on the lawn, a cypress-tree which he is said to have planted, is pointed out.

Pope was a premature and precocious child. His figure was deformed—his back humped—his stature short (four feet six inches)—his legs and arms disproportionably long. He was sometimes compared to a spider, and sometimes to a windmill. The only mark of genius lay in his bright and piercing eye. He was sickly in constitution, and required and received great tenderness and care. Once, when three years old, he narrowly escaped from an angry cow, but was wounded in the throat. He was remarkable as a child for his amiable temper; and from the sweetness of his voice, received the name of the Little Nightingale. His aunt gave him his first lessons in reading, and he soon became an enthusiastic lover of books; and by copying printed characters, taught himself to write. When eight years old, he was placed under the care of the family priest, one Bannister, who taught him the Latin and Greek grammars together. He was next removed to a Catholic seminary at Twyford, near Winchester; and while there, read Ogilby's "Homer" and Sandys's "Ovid" with great delight. He had not been long at this school till he wrote a severe lampoon, of two hundred lines' length, on his master—so truly was the "boy the father of the man"—for which demi-Dunciad he was severely flogged. His father, offended at this, removed him to a London school, kept by a Mr Deane. This man taught the poet nothing; but his residence in London gave him the opportunity of attending the theatres. With these he was so captivated, that he wrote a kind of play, which was acted by his schoolfellows, consisting of speeches from Ogilby's "Iliad," tacked together with verses of his own. He became acquainted with Dryden's works, and went to Wills's coffee-house to see him. He says, "Virgilium tantum vidi." Such transient meetings of literary orbs are among the most interesting passages in biography. Thus met Galileo with Milton, Milton with Dryden, Dryden with Pope, and Burns with Scott. Carruthers strikingly remarks, "Considering the perils and uncertainties of a literary life—its precarious rewards, feverish anxieties, mortifications, and disappointments, joined to the tyranny of the Tonsons and Lintots, and the malice and envy of dunces, all of which Dryden had long and bitterly experienced—the aged poet could hardly have looked at the delicate and deformed boy, whose preternatural acuteness and sensibility were seen in his dark eyes, without a feeling approaching to grief, had he known that he was to fight a battle like that under which he was himself then sinking, even though the Temple of Fame should at length open to receive him." At twelve, he wrote the "Ode to Solitude;" and shortly after, his satirical piece on Elkanah Settle, and some of his translations and imitations. His next period, he says, was in Windsor Forest, where for several years he did nothing but read the classics and indite poetry. He wrote a tragedy, a comedy, and four books of an Epic called "Alexander," all of which afterwards he committed to the flames. He translated also a portion of Statius, and Cicero "De Senectute," and "thought himself the greatest genius that ever was." His father encouraged him in his studies, and when his verses did not please him, sent him back to "new turn" them, saying, "These are not good rhymes." His principal favourites were Virgil's "Eclogues," in Latin; and in English, Spencer, Waller, and Dryden—admiring Spencer, we presume, for his luxuriant fancy, Waller for his smooth versification, and Dryden for his vigorous sense and vivid sarcasm. In the Forest, he became acquainted with Sir William Trumbull, the retired secretary of state, a man of general accomplishments, who read, rode, conversed with the youthful poet; introduced him to old Wycherley, the dramatist; and was of material service to his views. With Wycherley, who was old, doted, and excessively vain, Pope did not continue long intimate. A coldness, springing from some criticisms which the youth ventured to make on the veteran's poetry, crept in between them. Walsh of Abberley, in Worcestershire, a man of good sense and taste, became, after a perusal of the "Pastorals" in MS., a warm friend and kind adviser of Pope's, who has immortalised him in more than one of his poems. Walsh told Pope that there had never hitherto appeared in Britain a poet who was at once great and correct, and exhorted him to aim at accuracy and elegance.

When fifteen, he visited London, in order to acquire a more thorough knowledge of French and Italian. At sixteen, he wrote the "Pastorals," and a portion of "Windsor Forest," although they were not published for some time afterwards. By his incessant exertions, he now began to feel his constitution injured. He imagined himself dying, and sent farewell letters to all his friends, including the Abbé Southcot. This gentleman communicated Pope's case to Dr Ratcliffe, who gave him some medical directions; by following which, the poet recovered. He was advised to relax in his studies, and to ride daily; and he prudently followed the advice. Many years afterwards, he repaid the benevolent Abbé by procuring for him, through Sir Robert Walpole, the nomination to an abbey in Avignon. This is only one of many proofs that, notwithstanding his waspish temper, and his no small share of malice as well as vanity, there was a warm heart in our poet.

In 1707, Pope became acquainted with Michael Blount of Maple, Durham, near Reading; whose two sisters, Martha and Teresa, he has commemorated in various verses. On his connexion with these ladies, some mystery rests. Bowles has strongly and plausibly urged that it was not of the purest or most creditable order. Others have contended that it did not go further than the manners of the age sanctioned; and they say, "a much greater license in conversation and in epistolary correspondence was permitted between the sexes than in our decorous age!" We are not careful to try and settle such a delicate question—only we are inclined to suspect, that when common decency quits the words of male and female parties in their mutual communications, it is a very ample charity that can suppose it to adhere to their actions. And nowhere do we find grosser language than in some of Pope's prose epistles to the Blounts.

His "Pastorals," after having been handed about in MS., and shewn to such reputed judges as Lord Halifax, Lord Somers, Garth, Congreve, &c., were at last, in 1709, printed in the sixth volume of Tonson's "Miscellanies." Like all well-finished commonplaces, they were received with instant and universal applause. It is humiliating to contrast the reception of these empty echoes of inspiration, these agreeable centos, with that of such genuine, although faulty poems, as Keat's "Endymion," Shelley's "Queen Mab," and Wordsworth's "Lyrical Ballads." Two years later, (in 1711), a far better and more characteristic production from his pen was ushered anonymously into the world. This was the "Essay on Criticism," a work which he had first written in prose, and which discovers a ripeness of judgment, a clearness of thought, a condensation of style, and a command over the information he possesses, worthy of any age in life, and almost of any mind in time. It serves, indeed, to shew what Pope's true forte was. That lay not so much in poetry, as in the knowledge of its principles and laws, not so much in creation, as in criticism. He was no Homer or Shakspeare; but he might have been nearly as acute a judge of poetry as Aristotle, and nearly as eloquent an expounder of the rules of art and the glories of genius as Longinus.

In the same year, Pope printed "The Rape of the Lock," in a volume of Miscellanies. Lord Petre had, much in the way described by the poet, stolen a lock of Miss Belle Fermor's hair, a feat which led to an estrangement between the families. Pope set himself to reconcile them by this beautiful poem, a poem which has embalmed at once the quarrel and the reconciliation to all future time. In its first version, the machinery was awanting, the "lock" was a desert, the "rape" a natural event, the small infantry of sylphs and gnomes were slumbering uncreated in the poet's mind; but in the next edition he contrived to introduce them in a manner so easy and so exquisite, as to remind you of the variations which occur in dreams, where one wonder seems softly to slide into the bosom of another, and where beautiful and fantastic fancies grow suddenly out of realities, like the bud from the bough, or the fairy-seeming wing of the summer-cloud from the stern azure of the heavens.

A little after this, Pope became acquainted with a far greater, better, and truer man than himself, Joseph Addison. Warburton, and others, have sadly misrepresented the connexion between these two famous wits, as well as their relative intellectual positions. Addison was a more amiable and childlike person than Pope. He had much more, too, of the Christian. He was not so elaborately polished and furbished as the author of "The Rape of the Lock;" but he had, naturally, a finer and richer genius. Pope found early occasion for imagining Addison his disguised enemy. He gave him a hint of his intention to introduce the machinery into "The Rape of the Lock." Of this, Addison disapproved, and said it was a delicious little thing already—merum sal. This, Pope, and some of his friends, have attributed to jealousy; but it is obvious that Addison could not foresee the success with which the machinery was to be managed, and did foresee the difficulties connected with tinkering such an exquisite production. We may allude here to the circumstances which, at a later date, produced an estrangement between these celebrated men. When Tickell, Addison's friend, published the first book of the "Iliad," in opposition to Pope's version, Addison gave it the preference. This moved Pope's indignation, and led him to assert that it was Addison's own composition. In this conjecture he was supported by Edward Young, who had known Tickell long and intimately, and had never heard of him having written at college, as was averred, this translation. It is now, however, we believe, certain, from the MS. which still exists, that Tickell was the real author. A coldness, from this date, began between Pope and Addison. An attempt to reconcile them only made matters worse; and at last the breach was rendered irremediable by Pope's writing the famous character of his rival, afterwards inserted in the Prologue to the Satires, a portrait drawn with the perfection of polished malice and bitter sarcasm, but which seems more a caricature than a likeness. Whatever Addison's faults, his conduct to Pope did not deserve such a return. The whole passage is only one of those painful incidents which disgrace the history of letters, and prove how much spleen, ingratitude, and baseness often co-exist with the highest parts. The words of Pope are as true now as ever they were—"the life of a wit is a warfare upon earth;" and a warfare in which poisoned missiles and every variety of falsehood are still common. We may also here mention, that while the friendship of Pope and Addison lasted, the former contributed the well-known prologue to the latter's "Cato."

One of Pope's most intimate friends in his early days was Henry Cromwell—a distant relative of the great Oliver—a gentleman of fortune, gallantry, and literary taste, who became his agreeable and fascinating, but somewhat dangerous, companion. He is supposed to have initiated Pope into some of the fashionable follies of the town. At this time, Pope's popularity roused one of his most formidable foes against him. This was that Cobbett of criticism, old John Dennis, a man of strong natural powers, much learning, and a rich, coarse vein of humour; but irascible, vindictive, vain, and capricious. Pope had provoked him by an attack in his "Essay on Criticism," and the savage old man revenged himself by a running fire of fierce diatribes against that "Essay" and "The Rape of the Lock." Pope waited till Dennis had committed himself by a powerful but furious assault on Addison's "Cato" (most of which Johnson has preserved in his Life of Pope); and then, partly to court Addison, and partly to indulge his spleen at the critic, wrote a prose satire, entitled, "The Narrative of Dr Robert Norris on the Frenzy of J.D." In this, however, he overshot the mark; and Addison signified to him that he was displeased with the spirit of his narrative, an intimation which Pope keenly resented. This scornful dog would not eat the dirty pudding that was graciously flung to him; and Pope found that, without having conciliated Addison, he had made Dennis's furnace of hate against himself seven times hotter than before.

In 1712 appeared "The Messiah," "The Dying Christian to his Soul," "The Temple of Fame," and the "Elegy on the Memory of an Unfortunate Lady." Her story is still involved in mystery. Her name is said to have been Wainsbury. She was attached to a lover above her degree, some say to the Duke of Berry, whom she had met in her early youth in France. In despair of obtaining her desire, she hanged herself. It is curious, if true, that she was as deformed in person as Pope himself. Her family seems to have been noble. In 1713, he published "Windsor Forest," an "Ode on St Cecilia's Day," and several papers in the Guardian—one of them being an exquisitely ironical paper, comparing Phillip's pastorals with his own, and affecting to give them the preference—the extracts being so selected as to damage his rival's claims. This year, also, he wrote, although he did not publish, his fine epistle to Jervas, the painter. Pope was passionately fond of the art of painting, and practised it a good deal under Jervas's instructions, although he did not reach great proficiency. The prodigy has yet to be born who combines the characters of a great painter and a great poet.

About this time, Pope commenced preparations for the great work of translating Homer; and subscription-papers, accordingly, were issued. Dean Swift was now in England, and took a deep interest in the success of this undertaking, recommending it in coffee-houses, and introducing the subject and Pope's name to the leading Tories. Pope met the Dean for the first time in Berkshire, where, in one of his fits of savage disgust at the conflicting parties of the period, he had retired to the house of a clergyman, and an intimacy commenced which was only terminated by death. We have often regretted that Pope had not selected some author more suitable to his genius than Homer. Horace or Lucretius, or even Ovid, would have been more congenial. His imitations of Horace shew us what he might have made of a complete translation. What a brilliant thing a version of Lucretius, in the style of the "Essay on Man," would have been! And his "Rape of the Lock" proves that he had considerable sympathy with the elaborate fancy, although not with the meretricious graces of Ovid. But with Homer, the severely grand, the simple, the warlike, the lover and painter of all Nature's old original forms—the ocean, the mountains, and the stars—what thorough sympathy could a man have who never saw a real mountain or a battle, and whose enthusiasm for scenery was confined to purling brooks, trim gardens, artificial grottos, and the shades of Windsor Forest? Accordingly, his Homer, although a beautiful and sparkling poem, is not a satisfactory translation of the "Iliad," and still less of the "Odyssey." He has trailed along the naked lances of the Homeric lines so many flowers and leaves that you can hardly recognise them, and feel that their point is deadened and their power gone. This at least is our opinion; although many to this day continue to admire these translations, and have even said that if they are not Homer, they are something better.

The "Iliad" took him six years, and was a work which cost him much anxiety as well as labour, the more as his scholarship was far from profound. He was assisted in the undertaking by Parnell (who wrote the Life of Homer), by Broome, Jortin, and others. The first volume appeared in June 1715, and the other volumes followed at irregular intervals. He began it in 1712, his twenty-fifth year, and finished it in 1718, his thirtieth year. Previous to its appearance, his remuneration for his poems had been small, and his circumstances were embarrassed; but the result of the subscription, which amounted to £5320, 4s., rendered him independent for life.

While at Binfield, he had often visited London; and there, in the society of Howe, Garth, Parnell, and the rest, used to indulge in occasional excesses, which did his feeble constitution no good; and once, according to Colley Cibber, he narrowly escaped a serious scrape in a house of a certain description, Colley, by his own account, "helping out the tomtit for the sake of Homer!" This statement, indeed, Pope has denied; but his veracity was by no means his strongest point. After writing a "Farewell to London," he retired, in 1715, to Twickenham, along with his parents; and remained there, cultivating his garden, digging his grottos, and diversifying his walks, till the end of his days.

Some years before, he had become acquainted with Lady Mary Wortley Montague, the most brilliant woman of her age—witty, fascinating, beautiful, and accomplished—full of enterprise and spirit, too, although decidedly French in her tastes, manners, and character. Pope fell violently in love with her, and had her undoubtedly in his eye when writing "Eloisa and Abelard," which he did at Oxford in 1716, shortly after her going abroad, and which appeared the next year. His passion was not requited, nay, was treated with contempt and ridicule; and he became in after years a bitter enemy and foul-mouthed detractor of the lady, although after her return, in 1718, she resided near him at Twickenham, and they seemed outwardly on good terms.

In 1717, and the succeeding year, Pope lost successively his father, Parnell, Garth, and Rowe, and bitterly felt their loss. He finished, as we have seen, the "Iliad" in 1718; but the fifth and sixth volumes, which were the last, did not appear till 1720. Its success, which at the time was triumphant, roused against him the whole host of envy and detraction. Dennis, and all Grub Street with him, were moved to assail him. Pamphlets after pamphlets were published, all of which, after reading with writhing anguish, Pope had the resolution to bind up into volumes—a great collection of calumny, which he preserved, probably, for purposes of future revenge. His own friends, on the other hand, hailed his work with applause, Gay writing a most graceful and elegant poem, in ottava rima, entitled, "Mr Pope's Welcome Home from Greece," in which his different friends are pictured as receiving him home on the shores of Britain, after an absence of six years. Bentley, that stern old Grecian, avoided the extremes of a howling Grub Street on the one hand, and a flattering aristocracy on the other, and expressed what is, we think, the just opinion when he said, "It is a pretty poem, but it is not Homer."

In 1721, he issued a selection from the poems of Parnell, and prefixed a very beautiful dedication to the Earl of Oxford, commencing with—

"Such were the notes thy once-loved poet sung,
Till death untimely stopp'd his tuneful tongue.
Oh, just beheld and lost, admired and mourn'd,
With softest manners, gentlest arts adorn'd!"

In 1722, he engaged to translate the "Odyssey." He employed Broome and Fenton as his assistants in the work; and the portions translated by them were thought as good as his. He remunerated them very handsomely. Of this work, the first three quarto volumes appeared in 1725; and the fourth and fifth, which completed the work, the following year. Pope sold the copyright to Lintot for £600.

He was busy at this time, too, with an edition of Shakspeare, not quite worthy of either poet. It appeared in six volumes, quarto, in 1725. His preface was good, but he was deficient in antiquarian lore; and his mortification was extreme when Theobald, destined to figure in "The Dunciad," a mere plodding hack, not only in his "Shakspeare Restored," exposed many blunders in Pope's edition; but issued, some years afterwards, an edition of his own, which was much better received by the public.

In 1726, there was a great gathering of the Tory wits at Twickenham. Swift had come from Ireland, and resided for some time with Pope. Bolingbroke came over occasionally from Dawley; and Gay was often there to laugh with, and be laughed at by, the rest. Swift had "Gulliver's Travels"—the most ingenious and elaborate libel against man and God ever written—in his pocket, nearly ready for publication; and we may conceive the grim, sardonic smile with which he read it to his friends, and their tumultuous mirth. Gay was projecting his "Beggars' Opera," and Pope preparing some of his witty "Miscellanies." At the end of two months, the Dean was hurried home by the tidings of Stella's illness. He left the "Travels" behind him, for the copyright of which Pope procured £300, a sum counted then very large, and which Swift generously handed over to Pope.

In September this year, when returning in Lord Bolingbroke's coach from Dawley, the poet was overturned in a little rivulet near Twickenhan, and nearly drowned. The unfortunate little man! One is reminded of Gulliver's accident in the Brobdignagian cream-pot. In trying to break the glasses of the coach, which were down, he severely cut his right hand, and lost the use of two of his fingers, an addition to his other deformities not very desirable; and we suspect that Pope thought Voltaire (who had met him at Bolingbroke's) but a miserable comforter, when, in a letter of pretended condolence, he asked—"Is it possible that those fingers which have written 'The Rape of the Lock,' and dressed Homer so becomingly in an English coat, should have been so barbarously treated? Let the hand of Dennis or of your poetasters be cut off; yours is sacred." It was perhaps in keeping that those mutilated fingers were soon to be employed in attacking Dennis, and that the embittered poet was about, with the half of his hand, but with the whole of his heart, to write "The Dunciad."

In the end of April 1727, we find Swift again in Twickenham, where his irritation at the continued ascendancy of Sir Robert Walpole served to infuse more venom into the "Miscellanies" concocted between him and Pope, two volumes of which appeared in June this year. Gay, also, and the ingenious and admirable Dr Arbuthnot, contributed their quota to these volumes. Swift speedily fell ill with that giddiness and deafness which were the avant-couriers of his final malady; and in August he left Twickenham, and in October, London and England, for ever.

In these "Miscellanies" there appeared the famous "Memoirs of Martinus Scriblerus," written chiefly by Pope, in which he lashed the various proficients in the bathos, under the names of flying fishes, swallows, parrots, frogs, eels, &c., and appended the initials of well-known authors to each head. This roused Grub Street, whose malice had nearly fallen asleep, into fresh fury, and he was bitterly assailed in every possible form. Like Hyder Ali, he now—to travesty Burke—"in the recesses of a mind capacious of such things, determined to leave all Duncedom an everlasting monument of vengeance, and became at length so confident of his force, so collected in his might, that he made no secret whatever of his dreadful resolution, but, compounding all the materials of fun, sarcasm, irony, and invective, into one black cloud, he hung for a while on the declivities of Richmond Hill; and whilst the authors were idly and stupidly gazing on this menacing meteor which blackened all their horizon, it suddenly burst and poured down the whole of its contents on the garrets of Grub Street. Then issued a scene of (ludicrous) woe, the like of which no eye had seen, no heart conceived, and which no tongue can adequately tell. All the horrors of literary war before known or heard of—(MacFlecknoe, the Rehearsal, &c.)—were mercy to the new tempest of havoc which burst from the brain of this remorseless poet. A storm of universal laughter filled every bookseller's shop, and penetrated into the remotest attics. The miserable dunces, in part, were stricken mad with rage—in part, dumb with consternation. Some fled for refuge to ale, and others to ink; while not a few fell, or feared to fall, into the 'jaws of famine.'" This singular poem was written in 1727. It was first printed surreptitiously (i.e., with the connivance of the author) in Dublin, and then reprinted in London. The first perfect edition, however, did not appear in London till 1729. On the day of its publication, according to Pope, a crowd of authors besieged the publisher's shop; and by entreaties, threats, nay, cries of treason, tried to hinder its appearance. What a scene it must have been—of teeth gnashing above ragged coats, and eyes glaring through old periwigs—of faces livid with famine and ferocity; while, to complete the confusion, hawkers, booksellers, and even lords, were mixed with the crowd, clamouring for its issue! And as, says Pope, "there is no stopping a torrent with a finger, out it came." The consequence he had foreseen. A universal howl of rage and pain burst from the aggrieved dunces, on whose naked sides the hot pitch had fallen. They pushed their rejoinders beyond the limits of civilised literary warfare; and although Pope had been coarse in his language, they were coarser far, and their blackguardism was not redeemed by wit or genius. Pope felt, or seemed to feel, entire indifference as to these assaults. On some of them, indeed, he could afford to look down with contempt, on account of their obvious animus and gross language. Others, again, were neutralised by the fact, that their authors had provoked reprisals by their previous insults or ingratitude to Pope. Many, however, were too obscure for his notice; and some, such as Aaron Hill and Bentley, did not deserve to be classed with the Theobalds and Ralphs. To Hill, he, after some finessing, was compelled to make an apology. Altogether, although this production increased Pope's fame, and the conception of his power, it did not tend to shew him in the most amiable light, or perhaps to promote his own comfort or peace of mind. After having emptied out his bile in "The Dunciad," he ought to have become mellower in temper, and resigned satire for ever. He continued, on the contrary, as ill-natured as before; and although he afterwards flew at higher game, the iron had entered into his soul, and he remained a satirist, and therefore an unhappy man, for life.

In 1731 appeared an "Epistle on Taste," which was very favourably received; only his enemies accused him of having satirised the Duke of Chandos in it, a man who had befriended Pope, and had lent him money. Pope denied the charge, although it is very possible, both from his own temperament, and from the frequent occurrence of similar cases of baseness in literary life, that it may have been true. Nothing is more common than for those who have been most liberally helped, to become first the secret, and then the open, enemies of their benefactors. In 1732 appeared his epistle on "The Use of Riches," addressed to Lord Bathurst. These two epistles were afterwards incorporated in his "Moral Essays."

As far back as 1725, Pope had been revolving the subject of the "Essay on Man;" and, indeed, some of its couplets remind you of "pebbles which had long been rolled over and polished in the ocean of his mind." It has been asserted, but not proved, that Lord Bolingbroke gave him the outline of this essay in prose. It is unquestionable, indeed, that Bolingbroke exercised influence over Pope's mind, and may have suggested some of the thoughts in the Essay; but it is not probable that a man like Pope would have set himself on such a subject simply to translate from another's mind. He published the first epistle of the Essay, in 1732, anonymously, as an experiment, and had the satisfaction to see it successful. It was received with rapture, and passed through several editions ere the author was known; although we must say that the value of this reception is considerably lessened, when we remember that the critics could not have been very acute who did not detect Pope's "fine Roman hand" in every sentence of this brilliant but most unsatisfactory and shallow performance.

In the same year died dear, simple-minded Gay, who found in Pope a sincere mourner, and an elegant elegiast; and on the 7th of June 1733, expired good old Mrs Pope, at the age of ninety-four. Pope, who had always been a dutiful son, erected an obelisk in his own grounds to her memory, with a simple but striking inscription in Latin. During this year, he published the third part of the "Essay on Man," an epistle to Lord Cobham, On the Knowledge and Characters of Man, and an Imitation of the First Satire of the Second Book of Horace. In this last, he attacks, in the most brutal style, his former love Lady Mary W. Montague, who replied in a piece of coarse cleverness, entitled, "Verses to the Imitator of the First Satire of the Second Book of Horace,"—verses in which she was assisted by Lord Harvey, another of Pope's victims. He wrote, but was prudent enough to suppress, an ironical reply.

In 1734 appeared his very clever and highly-finished epistle to Dr Arbuthnot (now entitled the "Prologue to the Satires"), who was then languishing toward death. Arbuthnot, from his deathbed, solemnly advised Pope to regulate his satire, and seems to have been afraid of his personal safety from his numerous foes. Pope replied in a manly but self-defensive style. He is said about this time to have in his walks carried arms, and had a large dog as his protector; but none of the dunces had courage enough to assail him. Dennis, who was no dunce, might have ventured on it—but he had become miserably infirm, poor, and blind; and Pope had heaped coals of fire on his head, by contributing a Prologue to a play which was acted for his behoof.

Our author's life becomes now little else than a record of multiplying labours and increasing infirmities. In 1734 appeared the fourth part of the "Essay on Man," and the Second Satire of the Second Book of Horace. In 1735 were issued his "Characters of Women: An Epistle to a Lady" (Martha Blount). In this appears his famous character of Atossa—the Duchess of Marlborough. It is said—we fear too truly—that these lines being shewn to her Grace, as a character of the Duchess of Buckingham, she recognised in them her own likeness, and bribed Pope with a thousand pounds to suppress it. He did so religiously—as long as she was alive—and then published it! In the same year he printed a second volume of his "Miscellaneous Works," in folio and quarto, uniform with the "Iliad" and "Odyssey," including a versification of the Satires of Donne; also, anonymously, a production disgraceful to his memory, entitled, "Sober Advice from Horace to the Young Gentlemen about Town," in which he commits many gross indecorums of language, and annexes the name of the great Bentley to several indecent notes. It is said that Bentley, when he read the pamphlet, cried, "'Tis an impudent dog, but I talked against his Homer, and the portentous cub never forgives."

The "Essay on Man" and the "Moral Epistles" were designed to be parts of a great system of ethics, which Pope had long revolved in his mind, and wished to incarnate in poetry. At this time occurred the strange, mysterious circumstances connected with the publication of his letters. It seems that, in 1729, Pope had recalled from his correspondents the letters he had written them, of many of which he had kept no copies. He was induced to this by the fact, that after Henry Cromwell's death, his mistress, Mrs Thomas, who was in indigent circumstances, had sold the letters which had passed between Pope and her keeper, to Curll the bookseller, who had published them without scruple. When Pope obtained his correspondence, he, according to his own statement, burned a great many and laid past the others, after having had a copy of them taken, and deposited in Lord Oxford's library. And his charge against Curll was, that he obtained surreptitiously some of these letters, and published them without Pope's consent. But, ere we come to the circumstances of the publication, several other things require to be noticed. In 1733, Curll, anxious to publish a Life of Pope, advertised for information; and, in consequence, one P.T., who professed to be an old friend of Pope's and his father's, wrote Curll a letter, giving an account of Pope's ancestry, which tallied exactly with what Pope himself, in a note to one of his poems, furnished the following year. P.T., in a second letter, offered to the publisher a large collection of Pope's letters, and inclosed a copy of an advertisement he had drawn out to be published by Curll. Strange as it seems, Curll took no notice of the proposal till 1735, when, having accidentally turned up a copy of P.T.'s advertisement, he sent it to Pope, with a letter requesting an interview, and mentioning that he had some papers of P.T.'s in reference to his family history, which he would shew him. Pope replied by three advertisements in the papers, denying all knowledge of P.T. or his collection of letters or MSS. P.T. then wrote Curll that he had printed the letters at his own expense, seeking a sum of money for them, and appointing an interview at a tavern to shew him the sheets. This was countermanded the next day, P.T. professing to be afraid of Pope and his "bravoes," although how Pope was to know of this meeting was, according to Curll, "the cream of the jest."

Soon after, a round, fat man, with a clergyman's gown and a barrister's band, called on Curll, at ten o'clock at night. He said his name was Smith, that he was a cousin of P.T.'s, and shewed the book in sheets, along with about a dozen of the original letters. After a good deal of negotiation with this personage, Curll obtained fifty copies of P.T.'s printed copies, and issued a flaming advertisement announcing the publication of Pope's letters for thirty years, and stating that the original MSS. were lying at his shop, and might be seen by any who chose, although not a single MS. seems to have been delivered. Smith, the day that the advertisement appeared, handed over, for a sum of money, about three hundred volumes to Curll. But as in the advertisement it was stated that various letters of lords were included, and as there is a law amongst regulations of the Upper House that no peer's letters can be published without his consent, at the instance of the Earl of Jersey, and in consequence, too, of an advertisement of Pope's, the books were seized, and Curll, and the printer of the paper where the advertisement appeared, were ordered to appear at the bar for breach of privilege. P.T. wrote Curll to tell him to conceal all that passed between him and the publisher, and promising him more valuable letters still. Curll, however, told the whole story; and as, when the books were examined, not a single lord's letter was found among them, Curll was acquitted, his books restored to him, the lords saying that they had been made the tools of Pope; and he proceeded to advertise the correspondence, in terms most insulting to Pope, who now felt himself compelled (!) to print, by subscription, his genuine letters, which, when printed, turned out, strange to tell, to be identical with those published by the rapacious bookseller! On viewing the whole transaction, we incline with Johnson, Warton, Bowles, Macaulay, and Carruthers, to look upon it as one of Pope's ape-like stratagems—to believe that P.T. was himself, Smith his agent, and that his objects were partly to outwit Curll, to mystify the public, to gratify that strange love of manoeuvring which dwelt as strongly in him as in any match-making mamma, and to attract interest and attention to the genuine correspondence when it should appear. Pope, it was said, could not "drink tea without a stratagem," and far less publish his correspondence without a series of contemptible tricks—tricks, however, in which he was true to his nature—that being a curious compound of the woman and the wit, the monkey and the genius.

In 1737, four of his Imitations of Horace were published, and in the next year appeared two Dialogues, each entitled "1738," which now form the Epilogue to the Satires. One of them was issued on the same day with Johnson's "London." In that year, too, he published his "Universal Prayer,"—a singular specimen of latitudinarian thought, expressed in a loose simplicity of language, quite unusual with its author. The next year he had intended to signalise by a third Dialogue, which he commenced in a vigorous style, but which he did not finish, owing to the dread of a prosecution before the Lords; and with the exception of letters (one of them interesting, as his last to Swift), his pen was altogether idle. In 1740, he did nothing but edit an edition of select Italian Poets. This year, Crousaz, a Swiss professor of note, having attacked (we think most justly) the "Essay on Man" as a mere Pagan prolusion—a thin philosophical smile cast on the Gordian knot of the mystery of the universe, instead of a sword cutting, or trying to cut, it in sunder—Warburton, a man of much talent and learning, but of more astuteness and anxiety to exalt himself, came forward to the rescue, and, with a mixture of casuistical cunning and real ingenuity, tried, as some one has it, "to make Pope a Christian," although, even in Warburton's hands, like the dying Donald Bane in "Waverley," he "makes but a queer Christian after all;" and his system, essentially Pantheistic, contrives to ignore the grand Scripture principles of a Fall, of a Divine Redeemer, of a Future World, and the glorious light or darkness which these and other Christian doctrines cast upon the Mystery of Man. If, however, Warburton, with all his scholastic subtlety, failed to make Pope a Christian, he made him a warm friend; Allen, Pope's acquaintance, a rich father-in-law; and himself, by and by, the Bishop of Gloucester. Sophistry has seldom, although sometimes, been thus richly rewarded.

The last scene of Pope's tiny and tortured existence was now at hand. But ere it closed, it must close like Dryden's, characteristically, with an author's quarrel. Colley Cibber had long been a favourite of Pope's ire, and had as often retorted scorn, till at last, by laughing upon the stage at Pope's play (partly Gay's), entitled, "Three Hours After Marriage," he roused the bard almost to frenzy; and Pope set to work to remodel "The Dunciad;" and, dethroning Theobald, set up Cibber as the lawful King of the Dull, a most unfortunate substitution, since, while Theobald was the ideal of stolid, solemn stupidity, Cibber was gay, light, pert, and clever; full of pluck, too, and who overflowed in reply, with pamphlets which gave Pope both a headache and a heartache whenever he perused them.

Pope had never been strong, and for many years the variety and multitude of his frailties had been increasing. He had habitually all his life been tormented with headaches, for which he found the steam of strong coffee the chief remedy. He had hurt his stomach, too, by indulging in excess of stimulating viands, such as potted lampreys, and in copious and frequent drams. He was assailed at last by dropsy and asthma; and on the 30th of May 1744, he breathed his last, fifty-six years of age. He had long, he said, "been tired of the world," and died with philosophic composure and serenity. He took the sacrament according to the form of the Roman Catholic Church; but merely, he said, because it "looked right." A little before his death, he called for his desk, and began an essay on the immortality of the soul, and on those material things which tend to weaken or to strengthen it for immortality, enumerating generous wines as among the latter influences, and spirituous liquors among the former! His last words were, "There is nothing that is meritorious but virtue and friendship; and, indeed, friendship itself is only a part of virtue." Thus, "motionless and moanless," without a word about Christ—the slightest syllable of repentance—and with a scrap of heathen morality in his mouth, died the brilliant Alexander Pope. Who is ready to say, "May my last end be like his"? His favourite Martha Blount behaved, according to some accounts, with disgusting unconcern on the occasion. So true it is, "there is no friendship among the wicked," even although the heartless Bolingbroke, too, was by, and seems to have succeeded in squeezing out some crocodile tears, as he bent over the dying poet, and said, "O God! what is man?" His remains were, according to his wish, deposited in Twickenham church, near his parents, where the single letter P on the stone alone distinguishes the spot.

Pope's character, apart from his poetry, which we intend criticising in our next volume, was not specially interesting or elevated. He was a spoiled child, a small self-tormentor, full to bursting with petty spites, mean animosities, and unfounded jealousies. While he sought, with the fury of a pampered slave, to trample on those authors that were beneath him in rank or in popularity, he could on all occasions fawn with the sycophancy of a eunuch upon the noble, the rich, and the powerful. Hazlitt speaks of Moore as a "pug-dog barking from the lap of a lady of quality at inferior passengers." The description is far more applicable to Pope. We have much allowance to make for the influence exerted on his mind by his singularly crooked frame and sickly habit of body, by his position as belonging to a proscribed faith, and by his want of training in a public school; but after all these deductions, we cannot but deplore the spectacle of one of the finest, clearest, and sharpest minds that England ever produced, so frequently reminding you of a bright sting set in the body, and steeped in the venom, of a wasp. And yet, withal, he possessed many virtues, which endeared him to a multitude of friends. He was a kind son. He was a faithful and devoted friend. He loved, if not man, yet many men with deep tenderness. A keen politician he was not; but, so far as he went along with his party, he was true to the common cause. In morals, he was greatly superior, in point of external decorum, to most of the wits of the time; but in falsehood, finesse, treachery, and envy, he stood at the bottom of the list, without that plea of poverty, or wretchedness, or despair, which so many of them might have urged. Uneasy, indeed, he always, and unhappy he often, was; but very much of his uneasiness and unhappiness sprung from his own fault. He attacked others, and could not bear to be attacked in return. He was a bully and a coward. He threw himself into a thorn-hedge, and was amazed that he came out covered with scratches and blood. While he shone in satirising many kinds of vice, he laid himself open to retort by his own want of delicacy. He, as well as Swift, was fond of alluding in his verse to polluted and forbidden things. There, and there alone, his taste deserted him; and there is something disgusting and unnatural in the combination of the elegant and the obscene—the coarse in sentiment and the polished in style. And whatever may be said for many of the amiable traits of the Man, there is very little to be said for the general tendency—so far as healthy morality and Christian principle are concerned—of the writings of the Poet.

The Major works
Pastorals (1709)
An Essay on Criticism (1711)
Messiah (1712)
The Rape of the Lock (1712 and enlarged in 1714)
Windsor Forest (1713)
Translation of the Iliad (1715-1720)
Eloisa to Abelard (1717)
Three Hours After Marriage, with others (1717)
Elegy to the Memory of an Unfortunate Lady (1717)
The Works of Shakespear, in Six Volumes (1723-1725)
Translation of the Odyssey (1725-1726)
Peri Bathous, Or the Art of Sinking in Poetry (1727)
The Dunciad (1728)
Essay on Man (1733-1734)
The Prologue to the Satires (1735)